BUILDING BIG
PROFITS
IN
REAL ESTATE

BUILDING BIG PROFITS IN REAL ESTATE

A GUIDE FOR THE NEW INVESTOR

WADE TIMMERSON
AND
SUZANNE CAPLAN

WILEY

John Wiley & Sons, Inc.

Published by John Wiley & Sons, Inc., Hoboken, New Jersey

Published simultaneously in Canada

For general information on our other products and services, or technical support, please contact our Customer Care Department within the United States at 800-762-2974, outside the United States at 317-572-3993 or fax 317-572-4002.

Wiley also publishes its books in a variety of electronic formats. Some content that appears in print may not be available in electronic books.

For more information about Wiley products, visit our web site at www.wiley.com.

Library of Congress Cataloging-in-Publication Data

Timmerson, Wade, 1970–
    Building big profits in real estate : a guide for the new investor / Wade Timmerson and Suzanne Caplan.
        p. cm.
    Includes index.
    ISBN 0-471-64690-3 (pbk.)
    1. Real estate investment. 2. Real estate management. 3. Rental housing—Management. 4. Real estate investment—United States. 5. Real estate management—United States. 6. Rental housing—United States—Management. I. Caplan, Suzanne. II. Title.
    HD1382.5.T575   2004
    332.63'24—dc22   2004005523

Printed in the United States of America

10 9 8 7 6 5 4 3 2 1

To my supportive family, especially Sylvana and Pap
W. T.

To my extended family, especially Betty Caplan Liff
and the Timmersons
S. H. C.

CONTENTS

ACKNOWLEDGMENTS

The authors would like to thank their agent, Laurie Harper of Sebastian Agency, who placed this work in a good home; Sherry Truesdell, who kept the walls together until it was a completed work; and Deb Englander, who put on the finishing touches.

Wade is grateful for the expertise shared with him by Mike Wheeler and Paul Bergman of Coldwell Banker and the opportunities shared with him by Spencer Hirshberg. There would not have been a business had it not been for the love, support, and efforts of his parents, Wade and Jackie Timmerson, and the young man who motivates and entertains his father, Grant Timmerson.

Suzanne values the education of several experts needed for the writing of this book: Robert Danenberg, Esquire, and David Wilke, CPA. She would never have the time to write if not for the extra patience of clients such as John and Mara Roberts; Alan Cech, Esquire, a partner, advisor, and friend; and Tom Nunnally, a friendly agitator.

And finally, Success Productions has benefited from a number of those already mentioned and two valuable resources as well: John Walker and Dave Mackowick. We, and others who have learned from you, are grateful for your help.

INTRODUCTION

Wake up late at night or early in the morning and turn on a TV. You will see them: the sellers of books and tapes and packaged programs guaranteed to turn an average working stiff into a wealthy one, no longer slaving at a nine-to-five. Many methods are touted, some more obscure than others . For a while, it was owning a 900 number and enticing folks to call. The information available for the price of the expensive call didn't matter; profits would roll in. One problem: Callers began to complain to their phone companies as well as politicians, and this easy-money scheme dried up. Others inevitably followed.

Always present are the real estate gurus. Viewers can easily see the logic of investment in property. Even those of us who are complete novices know "real" people who have created great personal wealth as real estate investors. Some have lost money as well, but that story is seldom told. Regardless of the hype, this vast area of opportunity cannot be mastered by reading a single book, listening to a few TV programs, attending a seminar, or buying a few sets of tapes. The new investor has much to learn and many decisions to make. And then comes the additional education as they begin to practice what has been learned.

Chances are that your first real property purchase will be your personal residence. When you initially go out to buy the house or condo, you expect to pay close to market value. Your goal is to find the right space at a fair market price. You may even be willing to purchase a place that needs upgrades and repairs if something about it appeals to you. Your home may be an investment, but more important, it is a place to live.

To become a good investor, however, you must ignore personal preferences and go after property that is priced under its current market value. You must be as careful as possible to find homes or buildings that will need little repair. If the value is there in a fixer-upper, you need to be able to estimate reliably what the repairs will cost and do the work within that estimate. To succeed, you must make a number of these purchases and then rent them at positive cash flow or repair them for resale at a profit.

A successful stock market investor may need to do some in-depth research or may hire the services of a competent advisor, but becoming successful in real estate can be far more complex and hands-on. However, given the overall stock market performance of the last several years, real property can offer more security and, these days, greater upside profit potential. The value of a property *never* goes to zero. Even if destroyed in some catastrophe, insurance reimburses the loss. No reimbursement occurs in the case of a business failure; Enron, MCI, and United Airlines stockholders were completely wiped out.

What's more, with real estate, prices continue to go up even when the general economic condition is soft. They may just go up at a slower rate. The reason is simple: You can't create more land, so supply is limited. People always need housing, making the supply constantly in use. Ownership may change, but utilization will not.

Every day average people have a real chance to make some serious money in real estate. It requires taking the time to purchase good property to rent, or rehabing for sale and continuing to make new purchases that create growing equity. You don't need a lot of money going in. There are many creative ways to finance, from owner financing to hard money lenders—topics we cover fully in this book.

We explore the story of one investor who started fast, yet has made some mistakes along the way as well as a lot of really strong moves. Wade Timmerson, at the age of thirty-two, has built a multi-million-dollar portfolio of residential real estate in a period of seven years. He has purchased rental property and rehabs for sale. He also does exceptionally well at wholesaling or "flipping" properties. He now teaches and mentors others to do the same.

This book is designed to be an objective analysis of many of the aspects of real estate investing. We intend to encourage the beginner investors and to educate them as well. We are particularly interested in identifying the nontraditional investors, women and minorities who may be feeling a bit hesitant at the start. Whether a part-time or full-time participant, you can invest to increase personal cash flow and build equity for the future. The first deal is the hardest one to make, but you can't win if you're not in the game. And it *is* a game that anyone can play.

Suzanne Caplan

CHAPTER 1

STRANGER IN A STRANGE LAND

WADE'S STORY

The possibility of real estate investing interested me from the first time I heard about it. Even when I wasn't sure what to buy or how to pay for it, I was convinced that this field might be something I could master.

In the first place, my goal was to be self-employed. I was drawn to the freedom and the challenge even before I took on my first full-time job. More than that, I am a competitive person, and I like to be in the center of the action. You would expect that of an athlete, and excelling at basketball had been my drive since I was quite young. A bit small for a guard, nevertheless I made it to a small Division I school, and we played well enough to be invited to the NCAA tournament three out of my four years there. Confidence is a big part of my game.

Yet, once I had graduated from college and realized that my playing days were over, I had no real plan. Before I went to work for someone else, I wanted to try and go out on my own. My dad, who shared my dream, went with me to a business expo. We were amazed at all of the opportunities. Choosing one was hard.

I saw some great ideas but soon realized that the start-up costs were well beyond my means, so I went with a balloon venture, costing little and borrowing my dad's credit card to swing it. I eagerly read all the instructions and by the end of the next day, I had rented a kiosk at the mall and I was officially open for business.

I spent the entire day, every day, from the first of December until Christmas at the mall. I made a profit after all my expenses, but I decided that sitting at a mall all day wasn't what I wanted. Also, January sales would likely be far less than those over the holiday. I wasn't going to get rich here. No loss here except some of my time.

A real job appeared to be my only choice for the moment. My mother helped me land a job with the local gas company as a meter reader. As a teenager, I had worked part of a summer laying sod at a golf course in the middle of a hot humid July, and now I was reading meters in the middle of a February blizzard. I knew there was a better way to earn a living. It was time for another attempt at business.

Being a bit of a night owl, I often fell asleep with the TV still on and woke up hearing the late-night infomercials. The one about the riches of real estate always grabbed my attention, even if I was a bit skeptical. I listened to guys I worked with talking about buying rental property. They sounded as if they were doing well, but of course they were still working their day jobs. I was definitely curious and ordered a tape set "guaranteed" to make me rich. The minute it arrived, I listened to all of the tapes, but I still didn't get it. I'm not a slow learner, but I just didn't know how to start. So now I signed up for a seminar. Before I attended, my first deal came to me.

One day while I was at a house turning off the service after the elderly owner had moved to an assisted-living center, I was given my first chance to buy a house. The woman's daughter was worried about who would take care of it now that her mother was not there, so a quick sale was desirable. Hesitantly, I asked what she wanted and held my breath while she answered, "Thirty thousand." I knew the house was worth more than that, so I told her I would let her know as soon as I could. We made the deal at $28,500 even though I had no money and no idea what to do next.

I went back to my tape and books. According to the real estate guru, I was supposed to ask for owner financing, but at this point I didn't have the knowledge or confidence to ask. But I was in the game! I wasn't a sideline shooter like the guys I used to see on the court making all the shots but leaving when the pick-up game began. I played best under game conditions.

So I headed off to the bank and told them I had an agreement on a house worth $50,000. They said I needed $1,500 down, which was easy, and my payment was $220 per month. Sixty days later, I was the proud owner of the first house in what I hoped would be a growing investment holding. I was even able to go back to the bank and borrow another $10,000 to fix it up. My payment was now $350 per month.

Not long afterward I found someone needing a house to rent and willing to pay $550 per month, $200 more than my mortgage payment. If the gurus were right, this would be easy! After over five hundred deals, I still have that first house as a reminder.

The next deal was tougher to find. It didn't come to me, and I wasn't sure where to look. Back to listening to a tape and now off to a seminar on buying foreclosures. I paid attention, but I still wasn't quite sure what to do. That time and expense did not pay off. I was still reading meters and making plans.

Then I found my first mentor, a real estate agent willing to make the effort to teach me as well as sell to me. Mike Wheeler, a local Coldwell Banker agent, was patient enough to show me potential properties and help me determine their investment value. I'm sure I wasn't a profitable client in the beginning, but I know I've been one over the years. I've sent him many more clients as well.

Every type of investing, whether it's stocks, bonds, mutual funds or a more tangible item like real estate, has a learning curve. For the most part, the downside risk is less, but the range of return is greater as well. Unlike the market, where there is a fixed price at any given time, part of the challenge of real estate is that the buying as well as the selling price is always negotiable. Much of the money is made in the initial deal. Doing the first deal can be very intimidating. In fact, people running training seminars estimate that only 50 percent of the participants who take programs actually do any deals.

Doing your homework is the first step to success. Don't stop when you're through reading this or any one book. Minimally, you should be studying three to five other sources. A set of tapes may be a good idea as well, but you need not go for the highest price tape set. Some people learn more from listening than reading, but information is information. There are no magic tricks. Buying the most expensive program available won't give you any secrets—perhaps better sound quality and music, but no real secrets. Among the very profitable techniques, some are fairly easy to discover; the price of the tapes doesn't guarantee the quality of the information.

You will find the most expensive tape sets are sold in the back of the room at real estate investment seminars. The sets can be as high as $1,000 for a prepackaged product, and the free seminar is the hook to draw buyers in. Little information on the topic is given beyond the promise of how great the tapes and books will be. The material may be helpful and having tapes allows you to listen as many times as you need to absorb the advice, but the price is steep.

The seminars themselves range from small, locally organized ones to big, national mega-events. Those seminars that are free or very low priced are not really learning experiences but showcases for products and larger, much higher-cost products and boot camps, which is the current name for a three-day intensive seminar. These seminars can cost as much as $3,000 to $5,000. Hearing information live is a useful educational tool, and asking real-time questions can be very helpful. You will also benefit from the stories and concerns of other new investors. People face many challenges starting out, and more than one solution is available to each problem. Your choice of how many seminars to take, how much to pay, and how many days at a time you should attend should be based on your own financial ability and attention span. Perhaps you want to start out with less and increase the level of investment of time and money later on.

Clearly, the most valuable tool, but the hardest to find, is a mentor. Having an experienced investor willing to advise you about all of the aspects of your early deals can really make the difference. You may be able to find an interested real estate agent, or you may have a paid mentor program available to you. In recent years, as more new people have become property investors, some experienced players have established a reputation for themselves as professional mentors. For that service, you will likely pay one flat fee, usually ranging from $2,500 to $5,000, which covers a specific period or the completion of a specific number of deals. But beware: While some of these mentors are successes on their own, some are just wannabes, making money from selling services rather than property. Here are some ways to check out the individuals who offer this service.

Make sure that any mentor agreement is in writing and that you know exactly who the individual is with whom you will be working. In some cases, the provider is a company, but remember, the advice will only be as good as the person assigned to you. Your job is to ask for and then check his or her references as well, to determine his or her actual experience in buying property, landlording, rehabing, or anything else for which you feel you need close consultation. Question the person about how many units he or she holds or rehabs or deals he or she has completed. If you already have an idea what kinds of property you are looking for and where, try to find someone with expertise where you need it. No doubt you can make your money back on one good deal, so this is a good idea, but even more so if you work with the right person.

You may also be able to make money while learning instead of spending it. Some investors will bring on "bird dogs"—folks who scout property, get information, and then pass it on for the dealer to make the deal. You learn about what makes a good deal and may split the profits as well.

You will require the services of a number of other professionals on your real estate deals, including accountants, lawyers, and various money brokers. You may even need the services of a credit counselor. Eventually you will need to find all of these advisors, and locating the right ones in the beginning is a very valuable step. Interview several until you find some with whom you communicate well and who are interested in helping you build your business.

As you begin to evaluate the costs or benefits of any deals, you will want to know how your personal tax situation will be affected, so perhaps the best place to start is with an accountant who can act as your financial advisor as well. Owning real estate can help you shelter other income, and an accountant's help is invaluable here.

The first question to consider is what size accounting firm will work best for you. A sole practitioner may be overly busy at tax time and may not be able to meet your needs during that period. Larger regional or national firms have the most experienced tax advisors as well as younger associates to do daily work. They can help with sophisticated deals such as investment syndications, but you will pay expensive hourly rates for this level of advice. If your situation isn't complicated, this approach may not be required. A medium-sized local firm may be the answer. You need to investigate how much specific experience a firm has with real estate as settlement sheets (the paperwork you receive at closing) will have to be reconciled. As your holdings grow, you may need to install and operate specific real estate software, often requiring an accountant with real estate expertise.

Before you sign your first agreement, you should have it reviewed by an experienced real estate lawyer. The same question about firm size exists with attorneys. Sole practitioners become inundated from time to time, and large firms can be costly. Your early deals are likely to be fairly simple, but all contracts need to be checked for limitations and disclosures. The last thing you want to see is that the house you bought to rent out has been stripped of all appliances and lighting fixtures when you thought they were included.

Securing a clear title to property and preparing deeds and documentation for closings are the lawyer's job. You will be consulting one on a regular basis, so why not develop a relationship in the beginning? Real estate closings may be complicated, requiring some detailed documentation with regard to the status of buyer and seller, as well as the title of the property. An experienced real estate lawyer who is responsive to a client's needs is a valuable asset.

Are you making your purchases under your own name, or have you formed a business entity to be the investor? Are you familiar with business entities such as corporations or LLCs? Do you need a tax identification number, and do you know how to get one? These issues also require legal advice, and most attorneys can handle a simple business formation. If you are forming a partnership, make sure that both the legal entity and your operating agreement have been reviewed by a lawyer familiar with these transactions.

Your banker may be able to make a recommendation about professionals. The closers or other employees of a title insurance company see the local practitioners and know who are the most efficient. Don't be shy about telling your lawyer from the very beginning that you expect to do many deals over the years and want good service and to be billed at a consistent fee. A smart attorney wants to develop a growing client, so you both can prosper together. You may also get referrals from them and give referrals to them.

The next important player is your banker or loan broker. You will be making a number of loans over a short period of time, some of them long term (as in mortgages) and some shorter term (as in a line of credit). If you buy property to rehab and resell, the money you put into the construction may only be needed for a few months. While loans secured by real estate are fairly easy to get, a line of credit is a bit more difficult. Your personal credit history may come into play. A credit line is available funds that may be drawn on without additional approval. A number of the most favorable real estate deals are in buying properties that require quick closings. The buyer with the ready cash gets the bargain. Finding the best "money people" is your secret weapon.

Start by stopping in to meet your banker. Depending on the number and complexity of your deals, you may begin with a savings and loan, or you may want to develop a relationship with the commercial loan department of a larger bank. If the investments you make are logical, providing either good future profits or positive cash flow, they shouldn't be too difficult to finance. The earlier ones will take more time, but relationship building is about going back to the same source regularly and having the approval process expedited. Make sure you keep your records in good shape and maintain an updated personal financial statement.

Another professional service you may require is a credit restoration specialist. Your own credit score will determine how favorable a rate you can get, and in addition, at some point, you may need to work with your potential buyers in order for them to close a purchase. This service is a valuable one to rely on. You should know your own credit score and monitor it on a regular basis.

When it comes to investing in real estate, virtually everyone will tell you, "Come on in, the water's fine," but here's a caution: There are some sharks in the pool as well. When you are new in any field, your lack of sophistication may put you at risk. Some property wholesalers will tout high-risk investments, sometimes with higher-than-normal interest rates with the come on of "no money down." You will find many ways to finance investments with other people's money, but make sure the deal works regardless of the initial cost to you. You could end up holding title to a money pit.

The way to lower that concern and raise the chance and level of success is to learn as much as you can first and then find good resource people who will work hard to get and keep your business. Your own team of advisors may well be the best source of advice you can find. If you have chosen wisely, they will understand the value of shared success—yours and theirs—and they will make the effort to be there when you have questions. After all, down the road when you're up to speed, the success will be shared.

CHAPTER 2

DIFFERENT PLAYERS, DIFFERENT GAMES

WADE'S STORY

When I first started investing in real estate, cash flow was my main concern. All the gurus I had been listening to talked about positive cash flow. They described it as passive income. The numbers looked simple enough. As soon as I could match my current income with positive real estate cash flow, I could be on Easy Street. With my eye on that ball, I rushed to accumulate properties. Soon, I was a twenty-seven-year-old up to my eyeballs in landlording problems I didn't know how to or want to handle. Tenants even called me at home in the middle of the night over a crisis as small as a burnt-out lightbulb, and they were serious. The "passive" income did not seem quite so passive.

And there were the times I felt like a one-man collection agency, chasing after tenants who didn't pay their rent. My personal nature is not confrontational, and much of this was difficult for me. Over the years, I have continued to acquire and retain a number of rental units, but it only became comfortable for me when I was able to hire someone to handle the tenants and their problems. I have learned that I must file for evictions quickly for tenants who do not pay. I let the court deal with these situations, and my tenants are on notice that there are policies in place to handle them.

Another good real estate opportunity is finding property that needs work, making a good deal to purchase it, and then fixing it up to resell. It's called "retailing." Before I tried it, I knew all of the theory; I read those chapters and listened to the tapes. I still made every mistake along the way. I did my initial walk-through on my own, making a mental note of needed repairs, not writing down all of the details. I made my offer based on that walk-through before I brought in a contractor. When I did find one, he seemed to know what had to be done, so I hired him without getting competitive bids. I don't like getting bogged down in the details, and I'm not at all familiar with construction. The job that should have lasted five weeks lasted eight, and after an unexpected wall collapse, I was well over my budget and the project lost money. It was an expensive lesson.

I needed to be more careful and take greater time with this type of investing. My initial inspection should have included a contractor, and I needed at least three contractors' bids to compare. Attention to this process would have resulted in my showing a profit instead of a loss to my pocket and my confidence.

In one of the first seminars I attended, I learned about wholesaling, which is finding properties and selling them to other investors without closing on them. I didn't try it myself initially because I was focused on acquiring property to rent or to fix up to sell. Wholesaling transactions were more complicated, and I didn't know as many investors as I know now.

Then I attended a program completely devoted to flipping properties, as wholesaling is sometimes called. I took my wife-to-be with me because I knew how excited she would be after hearing all of the possibilities. I was right. She was ready to quit her job on the spot. We came home and worked hard for two weeks trying without success to put a deal in place while she was becoming increasingly pessimistic. Not me. I kept on working on what I had learned; my competitive nature wouldn't let me stop. Within the next two-week period, I had a wholesale deal, a property I then sold at a $7,500 profit a week later.

I have strong memories of my college coaches telling me to know my limitations and concentrate on where I have skills. For me, this meant to lead a team as a point guard and make everyone around me a better player. It's a lesson I frequently return to today. I still play to my strengths.

I continue to buy rental properties and try the occasional rehab, but my best skill is wholesaling. Now I rely on what I do best.

Most new investors go after rental property because of the cash flow benefit it can provide, not to mention the much publicized "cash out" check that looks like easy money. Both of these benefits are likely to happen but aren't guaranteed. That's why rental property may not be the right real estate investment for you. Remember, most of the "cash out" is drawing out the equity, raising the loan balance on the property and increasing the cost of debt service (monthly payment). Buying a property for a major rehab project that can result in a big payday may not be the best choice for an already busy individual who has no skills or experience in home repair. You should already know your own strengths. Being a landlord requires patience with tenants and some organization and management skills. Wholesaling would be a good choice for a natural salesperson. If you make a good match, you will increase your chance of success.

You want to begin by determining your own strengths. Are you organized, detailed, patient, or good with tools? These are some of the skills needed to become a landlord. You must be sure the property is ready to rent, maintain the records of income and expense, deal with tenants, and even do minor repairs to keep down costs.

Do you mind handling the constant contact of people looking at units to rent, as you will have to show vacant units from time to time to keep them full? You have to screen your potential renters, as well as take credit applications and check them out. The only way to minimize tenant problems is to screen carefully in the beginning.

You will need to set up a bookkeeping system to record rental payments as well as the outflow of cash for mortgage, tax, utility payments, and repairs. The only way to really measure the value of a rental unit is to keep exact records of the actual cash flow it provides.

Whether you personally live in a house or an apartment, you know that small plumbing or electrical problems inevitably come up. If you can't do the repairs yourself, you need to carefully manage the contractors you use to do them. One major maintenance problem can turn positive cash flow into negative outflow quickly. A new furnace can cost $3,000 and a new roof twice as much. Do annual checks of these and repair as needed. It's a good idea to keep a cash reserve on hand at all times to cover unexpected repairs. And remember, vacancies are a fact of life. Tenants move on, and you may even have to evict one from time to time. Cash needs for the property will continue, however.

Residential rentals are only part of the real estate investment business. Commercial properties are a large market as well. In some cases, there may also be mixed-use properties available with business property on the first floor and one or more floors of apartments available above. If you don't have experience as a commercial landlord, the best advice is to make sure that the apartment rentals cover all the expenses plus some cash flow.

Understanding commercial property involves some areas of greater expertise than most new investors possess. First, the credit decisions require some experience in assessing a business on the basis of its past performance as well as on future projections. Substantial cash flow can result from a successful commercial building, but serious problems can flow from your mistakes as well. Many commercial properties require leasehold improvements, which is money spent by the building owner to prepare the space and then paid back by the tenant over the term of the lease. A tenant who falls short can leave a landlord with both unpaid debt and a converted space that can't be easily rented to a new tenant. Space converted to accommodate a restaurant must find a new food service tenant or be returned to its original condition.

A quicker turnaround of profits as well as the most predictable return on your investment is an "ugly" house, one in disrepair that can be fixed and resold at a profit. Profits are speculative, so buying the property at the lowest possible price is critical. Always plan for more repairs than the ones you've factored in at the beginning. Take time before the deal is made to do a walk-through with a contractor you know well or who is highly recommended. Research the market values closely so you know what a mint-condition home in the area is worth. Put pen to paper, and then make your offer and stick to it. Many of the sellers you're going to deal with need more cash from their property than you can pay them. That doesn't mean you can or should raise your offer, because doing so could end up putting your money at risk. Once you have some expertise, you will learn how people can sell houses and keep more cash and which professionals can help them do it. All outstanding debt may not have to be paid off. Creditors may settle for less just to be paid.

The third primary way to make money in real estate is to wholesale or flip properties. Entire books are available on this subject, which is covered in greater detail later here. Basically you find properties that are priced for quick sale and which may be good investments for others as rentals or rehabs. You make the deal, get it under contract, and then sell or assign the agreement to your investor before you close to become the owner. You are paid for finding the property and nailing down the deal.

The real work in flipping is in marketing yourself so that deals are brought to you before going on the market. You also need good negotiation skills, and you need to discipline yourself to work in regional areas where you can learn the property values well enough to make offers on the spot. Profits on any one deal may be small, but doing a large number of deals is very possible as the time you spend on any one should be minimal. Risk is not very high either, and you will learn ways to keep them at almost nothing. The only money at risk is the hard money, and most experienced wholesalers offer little or no cash down.

If you have an open and friendly personality, flipping may be what works for you. Sellers need to feel as if they can trust you. Having a growing group of investors that you meet and interact with on a regular basis is also very important. To succeed here, you need to enjoy constant contact with people, some you know and some you don't.

Perhaps you are beginning to realize that becoming a successful real estate investor is not quite the easy game you may have thought from hearing all of the gurus. Learning and skills in a variety of areas are required: from record keeping to home maintenance to sales. The crucial first step to success is to choose the aspect of the field that plays to your strengths.

Your personal financial situation as well as your goals will also be a factor in the type of investment in which you specialize. If you have no cash reserve or little credit to draw on, you don't want to overextend yourself. A major repair or a few vacancies can create havoc with your personal budget. If you are already living close to your means, sudden expenses could cause real problems. Personal bills may be late, and your credit will suffer. Future borrowing can be at much higher rates or even turned down. Err on the side of caution. You can sell a property to raise cash, but real estate is far less liquid than stocks or CDs.

Your personal goals will also play a part in your decisions about real estate investing. How old are you now, and at what point do you intend to retire from your current work? Do you have children to educate or parents to take care of? Are you intending to spend the next ten or twenty years in your current location? Absent landlords can find themselves in trouble.

Being a successful real estate investor may not be as complicated as preparing for a career, but it is not as easy as just putting extra cash into the bank. You should know yourself—what you can and want to do—before you overcommit to owning property.

CHAPTER 3

SHOW ME THE MONEY

WADE'S STORY

Financing my first property was almost too easy. The bank made the loan as if they were making a standard mortgage, and my income certainly supported the payment. Even though the books, tapes, and seminars I attended kept telling me I could start with no money of my own, I wasn't sure exactly how that worked. I understood that you could ask the owner to finance the purchase, but I hadn't met any seller I would be comfortable asking. For a moment, after the first purchase, I wondered how I could go forward.

That's when I decided it might be a good move to find a real estate agent, so I called one that I knew slightly. Mike Wheeler, the man who became my first mentor, answered the phone at the local Coldwell Banker office and was very willing to show me some property to increase my investments. The first was a duplex that needed little work and was already rented at positive cash flow. I wanted it but admitted to Mike that I had no idea how to finance the purchase. He directed me to a small local bank that specialized in these types of investment loans. He even went with me to the appointment. Three weeks later, I was closing on that property. I was becoming a believer.

My first loan had been with the branch of a large bank and the second with a very small regional institution. There is a big difference: the larger the bank, the more paperwork and the longer the wait. However, one of the drawbacks of the smaller bank was the requirements for a 20 percent down payment.

Next step was solving that cash hurdle, and my new mentor showed me the ropes on this as well. We asked sellers to carry a 20 percent second mortgage, and a surprising number of them agreed. This was the key to quick property acquisition because I did not have to come up with much cash at closing. Still, doing this type of negotiating on my own wasn't easy for me. I wasn't sure what I would do if the owner said no. Once I realized many would say yes, my confidence increased. When I heard a no, I accepted it politely; if the deal was good enough, I figured out how to make it work.

I had heard the gurus talk about "hard money" (discussed in this chapter) as the way to fund deals without any down payments. The loan-to-value ratio was much lower than a bank, so you had to find really good deals and make sure the appraisal came in where you needed it. The costs are high—points at closing and higher interest rates—but the loan closes quickly, which allows an active buyer to go out and make a quick cash offer. I was soon buying three to four properties a month.

Hard money is used for the short term, so I could fix the property, rent it, and do conventional 80 percent bank financing. In those closings, I did walk away with checks, money I used to make new deals.

Each new deal made me a believer, and I began making purchases without an agent, not because I didn't value his help but I was learning that some of the best deals can be made on unlisted properties where agents aren't involved at all. I have developed good instincts about which sellers to ask for financing and which banks or other lenders to approach for specific types of purchases.

If you are saving or putting your money in any of the traditional investments such as CDs, money market funds, or stocks, you put up your own money. One of the most important elements with real estate investment is the ability to leverage your own cash and use financing to increase your level of participation. In some cases, you can get in without any money of your own. The challenge for the newer investor is to determine which financing instrument to use for each type of deal.

Perhaps the most important caution worth learning is that it is never a good idea to get drawn into a deal that is overpriced simply because you won't be spending your own cash. The deal may be appealing and the seller (often another investor) will try to convince you that the cash flow will be enough to cover the payment on the inflated price. However, any major repair or disruption in rental income could really cause problems: With cash going out and none coming in, and if the property is overleveraged, you won't be able to borrow to upgrade. If a deal seems too good to be true, it likely is.

Some individuals will let you purchase on a land contract. You pay them out instead of the bank. At a time when bank interest rates remain low, you are likely to pay a slightly higher rate than you might get from a traditional lender, and the seller would get the benefit from the higher return from these payments. You own the property and they own the loan. A variety of owner financing deals range from funding out the down payment to the full price. Often, however, you can negotiate price or negotiate terms, but not both.

Buying at a favorable price is important to any successful investor, and having access to cash to make the deal can really benefit you. A seller who is having serious cash problems or is facing foreclosure for missed mortgage payments or taxes, or that is an estate needing to liquidate the property of the deceased will be interested in a fast closing, and your access to cash makes you a desirable buyer. You may be able to pay 50 to 60 percent of what the property is worth for a cash deal.

The best place to have the ready funds is through your own cash reserve, where the profits you have made on previous deals are set aside as opportunity money. Make this one of your goals from the beginning. Another alternative is to secure a line of credit at the bank. You may be able to get one that is unsecured (requiring no collateral), or you may use the equity in your personal residence or the excess equity in your investment as collateral. Remember that this type of lending is for short-term use, so if what you are purchasing is meant to be a long-term hold (as in rental property), you will need to convert the loan to long-term borrowing. A line of credit is access to a given amount of money by prior approval, but most banks expect the line to be taken down to zero for thirty days each year.

Properties that do not need to close quickly can be purchased with traditional mortgages—one at a time. However, if you are buying a quantity of property at one time and you require a large loan, you will find yourself bumped up to the investment department of the bank. This experience will be different from working with the small mortgage lenders. Now you will be submitting information on the finances of your real estate business. By now you have probably formed a business entity, which will have a profit-and-loss record. This is the time when how you are managing your money comes into play. Have you made purchases (cars, trucks, equipment) or begun paying expenses from your overall company that are in excess of available resources? Perhaps you aren't drawing an income and think you are entitled to some perks. An astute banker will look at these line items, and while no one can or will prevent you from using some of your positive cash flow, your lender may be more cautious because of it. Review this with your accountant before you present any loan requests. You want to showcase your business in the best light.

Far too many new real estate investors start out doing well and get themselves too extended and into some difficulty. If you are turned down for a bank loan, consider it a wake-up call.

Another source of quick cash is what we've called hard money—a pool of money that private lenders provide to invest, and their main interest is the security of the loan. If you can get into a property and fix it up to rent or sell for less than 60 percent of its market value, you can find hard money lenders willing to do the deal for you. The cost will be higher than a bank both in the terms of points up front and interest rate. If the project is profitable, having access to money to make it happen will be worth it.

For example, if you buy a property worth $100,000 after rehab and you pay $45,000 and borrow an extra $15,000 for repairs, you will need to have a loan of $60,000. A 6-point closing fee is $3,600, and 12 percent interest for six months another $3,600. Assume that at the end of this time, you sell the property for $90,000—still 10 percent below full value. Your take is the price less the loan and the costs, which now total $67,200. Your profit is $22,800, even though the cost of the loan is higher than with a traditional source. But since you have none of your own money in, the return is described as infinite. Most investors would be very satisfied.

The cost of any bank loan is tied to the risk in the lending, which is determined by several factors: the cash flow of the property and the creditworthiness of the borrower. You should be already concerned with the first issue, and you must be aware of the second. Your personal credit history will be in play on a constant basis, and a poor one could result in a much higher interest rate.

In the very beginning of your investment career, you should take the time to check your own credit report. There are three credit reporting agencies, and you can purchase a report from each one of them: www.equifax.com, experian.com, and transunion.com. You can also log on to myfico.com and purchase all three online for less than $40. You will be asked several questions about your mortgage or open credit accounts to check your identity.

In addition to the details of your credit history and some other information, each agency will give you a credit score, which is based on a financial model meant to predict risk. The scores range from 350 to 850; the higher the better. Factors that go into this score include the following:

- How accounts are paid
- How long accounts have been opened
- Debt-to-income ratio
- Percentage of credit used
- Negative reports such as chargeoffs
- Number of credit inquiries

Several of these items are very self-explanatory, such as your payment history or total debt. Where real estate investors get into difficulty is in the area of debt-to-income, as your real estate cash flow will not be measured but your total debt will show. The other major area is in the number of inquiries. As you increase your level of financing, the number of times your report is checked goes up. This activity will not have a major effect on your score, but it will lower it. You need to track this, and you might need to explain it to any potential lender.

These days, you are not likely to have much personal contact with the decision makers at the large banks. Smaller community banks and savings and loans are different, and you will have a chance to get to know the loan officer. But whether in person or in writing, if you are aware of questions about your credit report, you should address them before you are asked.

You can also upgrade your credit with the use of a credit restoration firm. They review your report with you and challenge any erroneous reports as well as older derogatory information. Many creditors will withdraw this information rather than verifying. The techniques these companies use can add 50 to 100 points to your score. Check out the references of the firm you choose before you hire them.

Having a good credit score not only makes loan acceptance easier, but it will have an effect on your interest rate as well. The higher the risk, the higher the rate, and the difference can be substantial. Currently (early 2004), the interest rate for a favorable borrower would be between 5 and 6 percent while a higher credit risk may end up paying over 9 percent—a 50 percent difference! Think of interest rates as the cost of renting money. Why share more of your profit with the bank than you have to?

An owner who finances for you will likely be interested in who you are and how they feel about trusting you. A private hard-money lender will be interested in the value of your collateral, but a bank will look primarily at your credit rating.

Having access to capital to make good deals work is important. You will find a variety of ways to do any deal, but take the time to determine which makes greater sense. Lower prices are always desirable, but good profits can be made in leveraging other people's money. Take time to learn and ask questions of agents, accountants, and bankers until you feel comfortable with what you are doing.

CHAPTER 4

RETAILING

WADE'S STORY

I continued to buy rental property for quite a while, and my holdings were close to fifty units before I made my first try at rehabing or retailing a single-family house. From the time I made my first purchase, my main goal was to keep every property and to continue to increase my positive cash flow. I knew that I could shelter most of my profit, if not all of it, from income tax with the interest particularly, and with expense and depreciation deductions. I understood that if I sold a house at a big profit, it would generate taxable capital gains. I liked the thought of tax-free money. But after a while—making a few thousand in positive cash each month in my rentals and then putting it back into repairs in some of them—the prospect of a single big payday was looking better and better.

I do not generally chase after foreclosures, but one of my early and successful rehab properties was purchased from the bank after they had taken it over. I was not involved in the actual foreclosure process. It was a nice four-bedroom house in a stable neighborhood. Once I put on a new roof, did some work on the kitchen, put in carpet, and painted, I was looking at an additional $15,000 over the purchase price. I thought I could make at least that much in profit once I put it into saleable condition. The hard-money lenders who had been financing some of my rental purchases approved the project, which gave me more confidence. After my earlier misstep, I made sure to do my walk-through with a contractor in tow. After I had his estimate for the necessary repairs, I went to a second contractor, who actually came in lower. In the end, I decided it was safer to go with the original contractor I knew, pay a little extra, and have confidence in his work. The project went well and was done on time.

The best news was that I had the property sold before I even finished the work. By then, a substantial number of people who knew me from my athletic days, my utility job, or as social friends knew that I was involved in real estate investment. My phone was always ringing, and I kept a running list of all of the callers. A casual friend contacted me for advice about how she could go from her rental situation to owning a home. Of course, I told her about my almost-done project, and within weeks she was the buyer. Even after I gave her a $3,000 discount, I still made a $15,000 profit!

They all haven't been that easy. With one smooth deal under my belt, I thought I could repeat the process easily. I found a cheap fixer-upper in a borderline neighborhood, and I went for it because the price was right. Hard-money lenders came on board again, and the work was done by the same contractor, just about on budget. The problem here was that I couldn't find a single buyer who was interested in the area and could qualify for a mortgage. I eventually converted it into rental property. Even though it had positive cash flow, that wasn't what I intended for this deal. I was counting on cashing in on my profit.

I have had a few bad experiences where the repair costs went way over what I had planned for, but I can almost always point to my own failure to get adequate estimates and/or monitor the contractor as he did the work. When I do spend the time, I know the profits are there.

Buy cheap property, fix it up, and sell it at a profit. What could be better? While it isn't always quite that easy, the process can be very profitable. But there are a number of benchmarks along the way, and you must take care to analyze yourself at points during the project. Be disciplined.

You must make sure that the purchase price is low enough to leave ample margins for the profit you seek when you sell. You need to set up a checklist to follow when you look at property for the first time. Here are some of the critical elements:

1. Asking Price vs. Value after Rehab

Before you see any property, you need to know the range that the buyer is expecting. Is the property listed? Has it been on the market for long? Is it occupied? You should have some of these answers from the beginning.

When you first talk to the buyer, ask questions to probe how solid their asking price is. Find out from them about the condition of the property. Surprisingly, most sellers exaggerate on the negative side. If you find it worse than they described, you need to be extra cautious exploring other areas to find out what else they didn't tell you.

Then, check the current price range of properties in good condition in the neighborhood. You never want to have the most expensive property in any area. Get to know an appraiser from the beginning, and teach yourself how they figure out their comparison values (comps). The formula is to take a list of recent sales in the area and then, using the characteristics of the property they are appraising, add or subtract dollars to the price. A larger garage adds to the selling price; fewer bathrooms subtract; more bedrooms add, and so on. You make your own checklist. An appraisal is important to buyers when they are looking for a mortgage.

You need to keep your project—price plus improvements—to under 60 to 65 percent of the sale value in a restored condition. That goal will protect you in the rehab process and allow flexibility in a sale.

2.   What Type of Work Is Required?

There are basically three types of work that you can do on virtually any property. The first is cosmetic, which can include painting (interior as well as exterior), carpeting, and landscaping. Make sure you keep all of the decorating in fairly neutral colors. Everyone's taste is different, and anything too trendy could exclude some buyers. Making a property look clean and appealing will attract buyers, speed your sale, and add to your selling price.

The second type of work involves upgrades, primarily work on kitchens and bathrooms when they are shabby and out of repair. A fresh new kitchen may be a major attraction for a new home buyer, particularly for first-time buyers coming from apartments with small, cramped kitchens. A nice kitchen is a major selling point of a house. The work may be as little as applying a fresh coat of paint and new counter tops, up to installing entirely new fixtures.

You should be extremely cautious of ever undertaking the third type of work: structural work, which may include a new roof, or worse, a cracked foundation. On one hand, this needed repair may scare the owner into selling at far less than the cost of the repair, so you could benefit. On the negative side, you may find yourself encountering major problems, such as a ceiling collapsing or a wall or porch that gives way. You need the advice of an experienced contractor with these properties. You don't want to rebuild the whole house!

3.   Make Sure That the Area Will Attract New Buyers

One of the favorite real estate slogans is "location, location, location," meaning that these factors are the top three elements of property investment. An ugly house in a great location is a real find; an ugly house in a moderate location may still be profitable, but an ugly house in an undesirable area is far too risky, particularly for a new investor. All rehabs can get tricky. At any time, you may uncover problems you did not expect. Having a substantial margin between the purchase and selling price should cover you. However, when you find yourself in an area that is not attracting new buyers, you could end up putting far more into the property than you can hope to get out of it.

Focusing on neighborhoods you know increases your odds of success. Promote and advertise within the neighborhood, because people like to stay in an area that is familiar to them.

4. Hire Contractors Carefully and Pay Attention to Their Work

If you are going to do any property rehabs, the time to find good contractors is before you buy the property. The honesty and completeness of original bids and the speed and effectiveness of their work to the finish are key to your profits. Very few of us are experienced enough to question an add-on once work has been started, and that is the worst time to bring someone new into the project.

Give any new company a tryout. Let them do a small project that isn't critical, and watch closely how they perform.

5. If You Use Private Money, Consider the Cost

Many new investors are attracted by hard-money lenders because the loans are easier to secure and usually quicker to close. However, they are meant as short-term loans, so keep that in mind. A rehab that isn't selling quickly and has expensive debt can eat up a good bit of your profit. Keep the work progressing as fast as possible so you can minimize the impact of this debt service. The convenience of this type of financing works well in quick turnovers because the profit easily covers it. Anything longer than six months needs conventional financing. Set time goals for yourself to lessen your difficulties. Once you've converted short-term financing to a mortgage, you add a challenge to a sale.

6. Under the Problem of "Seasoning"

When a property is mortgaged for less than a year prior to a new sale, most banks are reluctant to grant a new mortgage to a buyer at a new, much higher price. This bank policy is meant to prevent the practice of churning property and raising its price for the purpose of withdrawing any equity and then defaulting on the loan.

If you are planning to rehab and resell in less than a year, get ready for some hurdles in having your buyer secure their mortgage. Prepare in advance by discussing the transaction with your banker and other professional advisors and documenting the increase in value you have added. If you've done some of the work yourself, keep your own time and material records.

Holding a second mortgage may also help in the solution of the seasoning issue. Once the first mortgage has been paid down a bit and time has passed, a full refinancing can be done.

7. Don't Be a Reluctant Seller

Put the property on the market quickly and advertise it aggressively. Know exactly what your total costs are, and don't hold out for every last dollar of profit. A real estate sale is always a negotiated sale, and some buyers just won't pay the asking price. They see that price only as a starting point in the game.

You don't want to be in a position to have turned down a good profit because you are determined to earn a "great" one. Consider holding a second mortgage as an incentive to your buyer. Profit deferred is still profit.

8. If You Have Few Offers, Convert to Rental

If you have spent a few months trying to sell a property that you've fixed up yet is still vacant, the next alternative is to rent it out yourself. You will need to convert your short-term lending into a longer-term mortgage. At this point, taking out the equity (the profit between what you paid and what it is worth) in cash even if you qualify for a larger mortgage is not a good idea. You need to be more concerned about cash flow. Find a good tenant, and you will earn money monthly and be able to cash out at a later time. A fully rented property will be attractive to another investor.

Retailing can make profits, but people who are really good at it specialize in it. Any investors, however, run into a rehab project from time to time, and trying it out doesn't hurt.

CHAPTER 5

LANDLORDING

WADE'S STORY

After I had acquired a growing number of rental units over a short period of time, I was expecting to receive the positive cash flow I had projected when I bought them, but it wasn't happening. I was usually covering expense and, of course, building equity—my long-term strategy for wealth. Most of the time, though, I did have positive cash. But then unforeseen events came, such as the day I opened my mail and found a water bill for one of my properties that exceeded $1,300. I was positive this was a mistake, so I immediately called customer service at the water company to discuss it. They agreed to send a serviceman out, and I arranged to be there personally as he checked over both the meter and the lines. We found nothing, but just as we were about to leave, a car pulled up and asked us, "What time does the car wash open?" It took a while for this to sink in, but the driver even told us what a good job they did. Sure—on my water bill!

At that time, I was so new at real estate that it hadn't even occurred to me to exclude my tenants from making any commercial use of my rental properties. And unfortunately, I didn't always take enough time to have tenants cover all of the utilities. I knew gas and electric could be high, but water wasn't even on my mind. That was an expensive way to learn a lesson, but I survived it, as with a number of others, along the way.

Any analysis of various types of real estate investments will show you that holding rental units is the way to long-term security. Once a building is paid off, the positive cash flow is yours to keep. If you've maintained the property, the appreciation in value is yours also. It's an investment that always pays a far better return than almost any other. Rental units always beat inflation and over the past few years have outpaced the stock market.

The challenge between now and then is the tenants. When I was starting out, I thought that the main problem would be collecting the rents. To be sure that I would receive the money, I would drive around and pick them up. I liked the thought of seeing my money, but I encountered unexpected problems. If I missed a tenant, they would not mail a check. Instead, they would hold their money and tell me that they were waiting for me to come back. My visits also gave everyone a chance to complain about dinky little things. They were getting to know me well enough to stop having any thoughts about calling me in the middle of the night over nothing. My wife was not happy about this new distraction in our lives.

In the early years I did not want to be thought of as a slumlord, so I overcompensated by giving out my home phone number and listening to all of the sad stories that were often offered instead of the rent payment, which turned out to be a serious mistake. I realized it when I began hearing the same story over and over from different tenants. Now I go directly to the magistrate after the fifteenth of each month and prepare to evict any tenant who hasn't paid. I've hired an answering service for off-hours calls, and my office takes them during business hours. They handle the problems, and few tenants have access to me.

I still want to treat my tenants as good customers, which they are, but I try to treat real estate ownership as a business, which it is. My mentor, Mike Wheeler, taught me, "Anyone can buy properties, but not anyone can keep them running."

A substantial number of new investors are concerned about being landlords. First they overcome their reluctance about dealing with property sellers, and then they have to deal with the issue of finding tenants. Many investors will only buy property that is already occupied, and some are willing to pay more so they can bypass the process of finding someone. Eventually, people will move out and you have to fill vacancies. Unless you hire a manager, you will have to learn the ropes.

You must start the whole concept of dealing with renting properties with the understanding that finding *good* tenants is the goal. You don't only want warm bodies who will pay a security deposit and the first month's rent and sign a piece of paper. Have a full application for new tenants to complete. Make them show several forms of identification, and then take the time to run a credit check and call their references, particularly any previous landlord, if there was one. Find out where they lived and with whom. Ask detailed questions of anyone who has moved on a regular basis. Many people move from time to time, but most of us prefer to stay in one place if we can. Were they evicted? Did they leave unpaid rent or damage behind? A few minutes of checking can help you avoid a real nightmare.

You must have documentation that goes beyond your lease agreements. You need to determine formal policies about when and how rent is to be remitted to you. Will you collect it on a certain date, or do you have an office where it can be dropped off? After what date is it considered delinquent? Where and when can a tenant call if there is a maintenance problem? You may even want to specify what is covered under your responsibilities and what is the tenant's—such as replacing burnt-out lightbulbs. It may help to make special arrangements that some work is handled directly by a contractor and tenants can deal with that person. List what day garbage is picked up and where they must place their containers. You may even want to recommend some local stores or restaurants. Be friendly and welcoming and at all times professional.

Remember, you aren't a massive real estate conglomerate. You are a local investor, and you need to look like one. Welcome your new tenants as you would any valued customer, and motivate them to want to be good citizens in your property. Showing respect may very well earn you respect.

The two things you want from any tenant are timely rent and reasonable care of your property. You're more likely to get what you want if you are viewed positively as a landlord. Making new tenants feel appreciated is part of the strategy. Being a strong but fair manager over the property is the other half.

Be absolutely strict on rental collection policies. Late notices go out even when "the check is in the mail." Begin eviction procedures for those tenants who go beyond the period. There may be times when you withdraw the action, but if you haven't filed it, you have lost the time. Tenants who don't pay and know they are on the way out are often the ones who do the greatest damage. The only defense you may have is to limit their time in the property.

Make regular inspections so if anything is deteriorating you know about it early. You should not, though, make your tenants think you are always looking over their shoulder. It is their home. Perhaps you can call ahead and ask if you can come by to look at a specific item such as the porch railing or the toilet that may have been leaking. Then you can see how the property is being kept, and you will be living up to your obligations as the owner.

You need to keep up on your own maintenance as well. The structure is your responsibility, and allowing the roof to leak or the furnace to get clogged will hurt you in the long run. Make a checklist for yourself and be diligent.

Paint when necessary, and replace any carpets that are becoming worn. These actions add to the sense of pride that your tenants will feel, and that will make them want to stay in the property and to behave.

You may want to consider using a management company at some point. Some investors do it at the same time they buy their first property. Some property owners never want to deal with any tenants.

The costs are not particularly high, usually between 6 and 8 percent of the revenue from the property. A management company can do as little or as much as you require. The firm can collect rent, make bank deposits, handle maintenance and repairs, take care of evictions, and just send you monthly statements and checks, or the company can handle only a piece of these duties. Some property owners want to be consulted before any work is done, but some give total authority to their property manager.

If you are fortunate enough, a good operation can save you a lot of aggravation. If you are just looking for one manager, be very careful. Make sure everything is spelled out in your management agreement, and find out specifically who does the work for the company. Does the managerial company employ maintenance staff or hire outside companies? Who are those companies?

You need to check references on any of the companies that will be involved in the handling of your money and your property. Verify bank accounts and references. If anyone will be doing work on your units, make sure they are fully insured. You are the one who will be responsible if anything goes wrong. Take the time and know who you're hiring before you turn over the property.

Rental units are a great way to build long-term financial security without having to continue to contribute large portions of your own income in an investment. Your tenants pay off the debt and leave you with a valuable asset that continues to pay a return. But rental properties are not a passive asset; being a landlord is work. Units must be kept rented and maintained, which can be time-consuming. Some subsidized rental programs can benefit you as well. The primary one most people are familiar with is Section 8. This program is covered in the next chapter and is worth your time and consideration.

CHAPTER 6

SECTION 8 RENTALS

WADE'S STORY

I grew up in a small town and went off to a local college. Then, once I went to work, I continued to live at home in a small western Pennsylvania town until I could afford my own property in the city. I wasn't aware of government subsidies for housing until I already owned a number of rental units and received a few phone calls from potential renters, asking if I accepted Section 8 vouchers. I was always looking for good tenant candidates, and when I learned that the rent would be paid by a government agency instead of an individual, this thought was appealing to me.

However, speaking with other landlords, I got mixed reviews on the program. Some claimed that all the eligible tenants would be trouble and would end up trashing my units. If that wasn't bad enough, they told me that the inspectors from HUD (Housing and Urban Development) force the owner to make major changes and repairs as a result of their annual inspections. There were owners who wouldn't even consider the program. I was a bit less enthusiastic.

Tenant damage is a very serious and costly problem in rental property. Even when you can keep the security deposit to offset some of the costs, the unit will be off the market while it's being repaired. Repair costs can add up quickly, so all investors, understandably, stay away from bad tenants. However, Section 8 program tenants have caused no more problems for me than non–Section 8 tenants.

Perhaps my success has come from the upfront effort I put in screening new tenants regardless of where their rent is coming from. Even though the money may be paid by a government agency, the people are the ones living in my property, and I am counting on them to keep it up. I let them know that. Some landlords just accept a Section 8 voucher without questions.

There are a number of reasons to like Section 8 rentals—even the yearly inspections, because they create discipline for the investor to check the condition of the property in depth and do preventative maintenance. Small problems can grow into major disasters if unattended, so this required review may be of value. Section 8 tenants tend to stay longer than others because once they've been approved by the housing agency and found a place, paperwork is involved in making a move; they can't just pack up and leave. You develop a better relationship with long-term tenants, and quite a few have rented from me while they were working hard to improve their circumstances. Once they achieved their goal, I eventually sold them a house!

Another benefit to the Section 8 program is a frequent overabundance of tenants—more renters than units. An investor who can provide housing within the pricing limits of this system will not have many vacant units. And most of these tenants will find their way to me, I don't have to advertise for them. That saves me money.

With Section 8 housing, I really like the fact that I receive my check in the beginning of each month from one source that pays the major share of the rental income that is due to me for a good portion of my units. The money is on time and dependable and recently has become an electronic transaction, making the reliability even better. I have had fewer problems with Section 8 payment transactions than independent renters. Once I familiarized myself with the terms of this program, the paperwork involved, and the expectations of the inspectors, I've had good success. I recommend it to other investors.

Any landlord who is dealing with low- and moderate-priced housing should explore the possibilities of renting under the Section 8 program. This HUD-funded program, which is administered through local housing authorities, provides all or part of the rent in the form of a subsidy paid directly to the property owner. You may find your local agency in your city or county. Eligibility is determined by family size (must be two or more related people), disability, or age (over sixty-two). Only the latter two categories allow for single occupants.

The program may not pay all of the rent, which is based on the income of the recipient (they pay no more than 30 percent of their income), and the rent reimbursement is set by the market value of rents in your area. So, if you have a two-bedroom unit that is extra large and might be rented at a premium, you won't be able to get that extra money from a Section 8 tenant, and the portion of rent that the tenant is responsible for will have to be collected from them. It is not guaranteed by the agency paying the primary portion. That collection can be difficult from time to time, but once you have a good working relationship with your tenant, you should be able to develop a system.

Virtually any type of property can be certified as eligible for Section 8 tenants, ranging from a single-family house to an apartment to a mobile home in some areas. There are initial inspections of the property to make sure everything is up to code, and these on-site reviews are repeated annually. You must also verify your financial soundness, proving that your mortgage, utility payments, and taxes are current. This step prevents unreliable property owners from taking advantage of the program and the tenants.

There is standardization in the rents; they are set at fair market value, and a landlord cannot charge more to Section 8 tenants than they would to other types of tenants. Nor can any extra money be charged to the tenant if Section 8 rent limits are lower than the market for the particular property. A landlord agrees to accept the allowable rent as payment in full. If you are caught collecting extra from a tenant, you will be bounced from the program permanently, and so will the tenant. They will lose eligibility.

Utilities can be handled directly by the tenant, if you have the ability to have them metered, and billed that way. This arrangement will be covered by your lease. While it is always preferable to have tenants be responsible for utilities so they don't overuse electricity, or other services, Section 8 tenants may present a challenge here. These are low-income families who may not be able to get credit from a utility company. You may have to work with them to set everything up. Section 8 will pay a portion of utilities as well.

Some additional work is involved when you first become a Section 8 landlord. You must make sure that you understand the paperwork requirements such as having properties inspected and making sure a HUD-acceptable lease is signed by the new tenant as well as having a signed contract with the HUD agency to authorize payments to the property owner.

Your potential tenant will have to be certified by the agency before the person starts to look for housing. Funding is not always available for the families that need it, so this eligibility certificate will tell you that your renter will be covered. The certificates have an expiration date by which a lease must be executed. Tenants who do not find property by this date are no longer covered. Make sure you track this, as it is the only way to assure you will be paid. You will issue a document once you have accepted a tenant to lock in the arrangement. Typically, there is a 60-day window.

Some tenants must pay part of the rent themselves, as a result of their income level. You should know this before you sign a lease, and make your credit decision as you would with a private-paying tenant. Also, remember that if someone's income is low enough to make them qualify for Section 8, that doesn't mean that he or she is financially unreliable. The problems may be short term or caused by circumstances outside of the individual's control. People from all income levels find themselves overextended, and some face their problems and deal with them while others avoid responsibility. Make your judgments on character, not wealth. In difficult economic conditions, all kinds of people can be under financial stress.

Eligibility may change as income level changes, and you need to track this as well. Families can stay in the program as long as they need the assistance, but their eligibility will have to be renewed each year. Your rental subsidy payments will stop at the end of the lease term unless this recertification has been done. It's more than a matter of having a lease renewal signed. Track your dates carefully.

Eligibility can also be withdrawn if there has been any misreporting of income. You will be notified if this violation has happened. You don't have to evict the tenants, but they will have to pay their own rent. Having residents in the property and not on the lease can also result in benefits being withdrawn. Any criminal activity such as illegal drug use will also be dealt with by losing the subsidy.

You retain all of your rights as a landlord when you are renting to Section 8 tenants. If they do not pay their portion of the rent or if they become a nuisance, you can file any action that is permitted by your state or local courts. Any damage done to your property by a Section 8 tenant will be charged to the resident. Whether or not the tenant has paid for them, the repairs must be done because the unit must be kept up to code. All or part of these costs may be reimbursed. Check with your local Section 8 agency to determine these procedures.

You may be able to make a claim for lost rent in the event that an eligible tenant vacates the property during their lease. You must make a timely claim, usually within sixty days, and you must make an effort to rent the unit as soon as you can and retain proof that you have done so. Given the abundance of Section 8–eligible candidates, your property should not be empty for long.

If your expenses with the property rise, such as higher taxes or utility bills, you can pass that increase along to the agency providing the subsidy. Make sure that you do so at least sixty days prior to the renewal date of the lease, and be specific about the reasons for your request. You are dealing with a bureaucracy, and you need to provide them with all of the paperwork, no matter what you are trying to accomplish. Learn this early, and everything will work much more smoothly. But Section 8 rents go up as private rents go up.

You are not prevented from selling your property while it is under contract to Section 8 and leased to eligible renters, but those leases and agreements will stay in effect for the new owner who must honor the balance of any existing agreements. In many instances, this will be a desirable feature for a new owner, particularly a new investor. The cash flow will already be in place from a reliable source. You know exactly when the money will arrive to pay the rent, and government checks never bounce.

Other agencies may provide housing assistance, such as the Salvation Army and church-sponsored community charities that service disabled or older citizens. Some of these programs are underwritten by HUD money, and some may be denomination- or foundation-supported. Income guidelines are normally the same as Section 8, as are the market value rents. Paperwork requirements are normally the same as well.

You have responsibilities as a Section 8 landlord: paperwork, maintenance, and tenant management. You have benefits under Section 8 as well: a ready supply of tenants and a reliable source of rent payments. If you finance a property on a fifteen-year mortgage and rent it to a long-term tenant, you will find yourself with a free and clear title sooner than you think. Like all rentals, you will have the cash flow plus the value of increase in equity. The final benefit is in being able to provide good housing to good people who are having difficult times. The content of one's wallet is not an indication of the content of one's character.

CHAPTER 7

THE WHOLESALE GAME

WADE'S STORY

As in the case with most new investors, my early venture into real estate was buying rental properties. I found it easy to understand this as the way to build long-term wealth, and I was careful to make sure all of my properties had positive cash flow—that the rent I collected exceeded the mortgage, tax, and utility payments. But that never seemed to put enough cash in my pocket, particularly while I continued in the buying mode. I was paying closing costs for new property as well as the occasional costly repair. I tried the rehab (or retailing) side, looking for a big payday, and I had one from time to time. I lost money at times. But it could take six to nine months to cash out of a property, and I was looking for faster and larger cash flow.

That's what motivated me to spend yet another $2,500 on a "boot camp," this time one that was dedicated to wholesaling, also known as flipping properties. After that, it only took a few weeks of looking, and once I had my first $7,500 in profit (on one deal!), I was hooked. Wholesaling is now the bread-and-butter of my business, and in the last five years, I've flipped about four hundred houses. The deals come to me in greater quantity now than they did in the beginning. Good times and bad, houses change hands. My job is to find them before anyone else does and to get them under my control with a contract.

The first part of the transaction is to "buy" the property—that is, get it under agreement. I specialize in low- to moderate-cost housing, and I find that these properties are often ignored by the typical real estate agent. When you consider how many ways they have to split their commission, it isn't surprising. The payoff is small, and the work can be hard because many times, the buyers of houses in this range need a lot of hand holding to secure a mortgage.

I don't put up any billboards (though they can be very effective), but I do have signs on my truck, pass out a lot of "I buy houses" business cards, send out direct mail pieces, and advertise in the paper. The more people who know me and know what I do, the greater the number of referrals that I receive. This name recognition is the most critical element of my success.

One of the most satisfying aspects of this work is that I am often solving someone's problem at the same time I am making money. It may be the family of an elderly person going to a care facility and vacating a house or people who are over their heads in debt and need to consolidate. I can get them out from under a mortgage and often put cash in their pockets.

I usually know during the first phone contact whether I can make a deal or not. Because I work in areas that are familiar to me, I have a good idea of what the property is worth. If the seller is looking for too much money, I can't make a deal and I don't waste either of our time in pointless conversation. If the seller seems open to negotiation, I will spend more time trying to make an offer that will fit.

The term "flipping" comes from the fact that a property is

turned over (or flipped) to another investor quickly, before the original sale has closed. It takes some time in the business to develop a group of eager buyers, but once you've located some good deals for a few investors, word spreads. Some of them don't have the time to spend to locate good property, so I am of value to them. We both profit from the deal. Because no agent is involved, savings occurs on the absence of any real estate commission. These days, eager new investors are always lining up.

My profit on each deal is usually between $3,000 and $5,000, not bad for a few hours of work, but I have made as much as $38,000 on a single transaction. It started with a call from out of town that gave me the chance to buy a property in bad shape but in a great area. Parents had moved in with their children in another state, and the property was vacant. Their daughter wanted out from under any more responsibility for the property. They had not been able to rent the house since the last tenants moved, and she knew it had been trashed. I quickly signed a sales agreement and listed the property on my website. Then I sent someone over to haul out all of the junk that was in virtually every room. Within two days, I had five buyers ready to take the deal. I had a great payday. The seller was grateful on top of it!

A number of techniques are available to making profits at wholesaling properties, but the most important is being the one to find the deal and get it under agreement. The investor is paying you to do the legwork and make the initial deal, so you have to spend time and effort on this pursuit. That process begins with your own education. You need to have strong knowledge of housing values so you can make an offer on the spot to the buyer.

Most properties that come in this category are distressed sales sold for unhappy reasons, often one of the three Ds:

- Divorce
- Debt
- Death

Other reasons for a quick sale are absentee owners and investors who decide that the time and effort isn't worth it. Often what precipitates this change of heart is one or more extended vacancies or some experience with nightmare tenants or major repair expense. A new investor is always more optimistic.

Your challenge is to find these motivated sellers by one of a variety of methods. Using more than one is a good strategy. The more properties you locate, the greater the possibility of finding the bargains and making a wholesale deal. Here are some places to start.

- ### Call Newspaper Ads "For Rent"

One of the major selling motivators is vacant property, so you may find an owner who would be relieved to sell a vacant house. Perhaps the property is not owned by an investor but by someone who has moved out of the area or has needed to relocate a parent out of their family home. Ask if the person might be interested in selling instead of renting. Leave your name and phone number. The longer it is vacant, the more motivated the owner might be.

- ### Check Out FSBOs

"For Sale by Owner" means that no real estate agent is involved, which may happen for a variety of reasons. Some properties are never listed because the owner does not want to pay a commission. The property may have been listed and not sold during the listing period, or it may be that disgruntled investor we discussed. Pay particular attention to ads that describe a fixer-upper or handyman's special, or the words "needs work." The owner, in this case, knows he or she has a problem sale on their hands. You may be just what the owner is looking for.

• Do Your Own Advertising

A "We Buy Houses" ad almost always gets a call. Real estate changes hands on a regular basis, and an owner likely to sell may review the want ads before placing his or her own. It is always a good sign when your phone is ringing with sellers looking for offers. The more opportunities you have, the more deals you are likely to make.

• Ask Your Banker

If you have a relationship with a small community banker, you may be able to find out about estate sales or newly motivated buyers. Your banker is unlikely to tell you the reason for this motivation, but you may be clued into a property that is about to come on the market. This is the best time to find out—before anyone else. Insurance agents may also be a source of referrals, as are lawyers, particularly those who handle estates.

• Drive Around the Neighborhood

You should be taking an occasional drive around any familiar areas looking for signs by owners of a property for rent or for sale. Vacant properties may have motivated sellers owning them. Many FSBOs are not advertised in the paper. Attend any owner open houses. They offer a good way to market yourself, and you just might be able to find a bargain.

• Do Direct Mail

You can create a postcard to send as a marketing piece for very little money, and you will find them to be quite effective. Perhaps you can begin with one that is as generic as a "We Buy Houses" piece and also one that is specifically directed to owners of vacant properties. Let them know that you can help end the expense of owning an empty house. They are paying taxes and utilities in addition to a mortgage—money out and no money in.

Print these cards on brightly colored card stock and send them out on a regular basis. Perhaps send fifty each week to a mailing list of a particular area. You can buy the list from a mailing house at a reasonable cost. Carry the "vacant property" card in your car. When you see an empty house, address the prestamped card to "occupant" and put it in the nearest USPS mailbox.

- **Ask for Referrals**

When you have bought a house from someone, whatever the reason they are selling, thank them for the deal. Ask them to give your name to anyone else who might be looking to sell a house. A satisfied seller is the best salesperson you can have.

- **Market Yourself and What You Do**

Putting a face and a person behind any business is always a good idea. That's why big corporations often turn to a spokesperson such as Wendy's Dave Thomas. Keep a high public profile.

Join a variety of business organizations, and attend the meetings as often as you can. Try your local Chamber of Commerce. At gatherings, hand out as many cards as possible. You might even want to leave them behind. The more people who remember your name and face and think of it when someone mentions selling a house, the more callers you will get. This business benefits from a high profile. Choose a catchy name for your business, and make sure your company is listed in the phone book. Consider a display ad in the Yellow Pages.

LEARN HOW TO NEGOTIATE

Finding the property for sale is step one. The next step is to know how much it is worth and the maximum offer you can make. Experienced wholesalers can do the entire transaction on the phone. Beginners cannot.

Visit the property and take notes on the condition of the structure as well as the neighborhood. Whether used by your buyer as a rental or as a rehab and then sold, someone will be living there. Make sure the environment is habitable. Low price is not the main goal. Good value is.

Ask questions of the owner to determine what they expect as well as what they need. Let them know that your offer is the maximum an investor can make, not what you think the value is. You are trying to solve their problem, not insult them. The more deals you do, the easier the negotiations will be. If a deal isn't working, walk away from it. Don't overcompensate to please the seller. Make sure you do an on-site inspection when you can.

HAVE A SIGNED AGREEMENT

Several elements are critical in a wholesale agreement. You want the name of the buyer to be you (or your company) and the term "and/or assigns." These words give you the ability to sell the rights to this purchase without ever closing. This clause is the critical element of any property flipping. Your deal should be closed by your investor, not by you. Your fee is an add-on to the buyer—the price they will pay. Explain this deal to the seller up-front, or you may encounter a possible glitch in your closing.

You do not want to give any earnest money at all; if you must, make it a token amount, such as $100. The seller may question this, but you can explain that as an investor, you can't put hard money on the ten to twenty deals you make a month. If you are absolutely sure of the deal, you can make an exception, but keep it as low as you can.

Finally, make sure that the terms of the agreement limit your loss to the forfeiture of any hard money in any failure to close. Sometimes a deal simply won't close, and you don't want to leave yourself open to any lawsuits. Be open with your sellers. Help them understand the role of an investor. You will not be the eventual owner. You are being paid a finders fee for making the match.

LINE UP YOUR BUYERS

As an active wholesaler, you will want to develop and maintain contact with as large a group of investors as you can. In the beginning, you may find them through newspaper ads and local real estate groups. Slowly you should be building up a database of known interested investors, and you should include their preferences. Many will concentrate on particular neighborhoods or types of properties—single-family or multiple units. Some may be looking for some hardcore handyman specials; the bigger the challenge, the more they like it.

The minute you find a property to place under contract, begin to market it. The more interest you can generate, the better. Because the closing will normally take place in thirty days or less, your investor/buyer will need to line up their own financing quickly. A good find should not have to stay on the market for long.

The last piece of this puzzle before payday is the closing. You will have some responsibility making sure that all of the paperwork is complete and that the closing attorney is preparing the documentation on a timely basis. The seller will look to you and will be very stressed if a problem arises during this sale. Be sympathetic and professional even if this deal is only a small fee for you.

CHAPTER 8

DOING WELL BY DOING GOOD

WADE'S STORY

I enjoy so many things about real estate, especially the fact that no two days are the same and that all of the deals I make are different. I am never bored. I spend a good deal of time in my car exploring, and I can pull off some very profitable transactions that are really satisfying, but some of the best experiences I have are working with people and solving their problems. I make money, and they are thrilled. What a shared win!

My first rent-to-own sale was one of those special deals. The call came from a couple in their fifties whom a mortgage broker referred to me. They had been renters all of their lives, but as a result of some recent neighborhood violence that resulted in a serious injury to their son, they wanted a safer home and had hoped for ownership. Unfortunately, they did not qualify for the initial deal they wanted to make. That's when I was introduced to them.

I was able to find a desirable home to rent to this couple. I had only paid in the 40s, but it was worth much more. They gave me some money down, and I signed a lease with them that allowed them to convert this rental into a buy and to receive credit for some of the money paid as rent along the way.

It eventually took eighteen months to clear their credit. They paid down on some debts and challenged some others, but we did secure mortgage financing. I earned almost $15,000 on the deal and they lowered their monthly payments by almost $100 a month, and most importantly, they were the owners!

I could see their pride at the closing. This was a lifelong dream, and I had a hand in making it happen. They thanked me time and time again and even promised to buy me dinner! I have done over a hundred of these deals, and it is always a happy event. I have received gifts and cards and am still remembered during the holidays, years after the sale.

Rent-to-own tenants are abundant. Home ownership remains an American Dream, but several hurdles must be cleared for people who haven't done it before. In some cases, job histories are erratic and not easily verifiable. In others, credit may be nonexistent or negative. Both of these situations are correctable, but it takes effort beyond just being a landlord to do so. I describe it as "advanced landlording." This strategy has proven successful for me.

I screen rent-to-own tenants more carefully than my other renters, although I am generally careful about anyone who moves into my property. I not only check their credit, but I sit down and carefully explain what it is going to take to own their home. I tell them that this process will require effort as well as a commitment of both money and time.

I require a down payment of at least $2,000 or approximately 3 percent of the purchase price. This is nonrefundable, credited to the down payment when we close the deal but forfeited if we don't.

Then I work on the issue of securing a mortgage, which likely has been the main problem. I have a few strategies that I employ here. One is to make sure all rent is paid by check, which establishes a payment history. Having a bank account and record of current rent payments is necessary for verification.

I discovered, after a few of my early clients failed to secure a mortgage, that using a good credit restoration program increased the success rate substantially. I require my rent-to-own clients to enroll in this type of program before they take possession of the home. They get help from a professional in learning where their problem areas are and what has to be done before they can qualify for a mortgage. I have seen credit scores go up by over one hundred points in a short amount of time, and I have had tenants become owners in less than six months.

I receive calls and e-mails all of the time from people asking for help to buy a home of their own. When I find one who is motivated, I am more than happy to work with them to make this happen. This scores a win for the investor in every way.

Buying property and then renting it to an eventual buyer may be a very good deal for some investors, but not all. If you are investing for the long term, this isn't the right strategy because you will be constantly buying or selling property. While the profit is there, so are the tax implications. Depending on how long you hold a property, the profits you make may likely be taxed at the rate of any ordinary income. You decide whether you are looking for cash flow or long-term appreciation. While very little is completely passive about real estate investing, buying property to sell as a rent-to-own is certainly one of the more active areas.

BEGIN BY LOCATING GOOD PROPERTY

As in any form of investing, finding the right property to purchase is a key to your ultimate success. In this case, you begin by finding property that is of good value, but also in a low-to-very-moderate price range. The typical rent-to-own candidate likely has limited income (although there are exceptions), so the total cost to be mortgaged must be fairly low. Some parts of the country have very little housing that can be used for this purpose, or you must go too far outside of the city environment to find it. Getting into more rural areas may make transportation to a job a difficulty for potential buyers. Inner-city areas remain the most fertile ground. Older suburbs can also be a reasonable place to look for candidates.

If you are located in one of the cities that has an abundance of stable yet low-cost housing, selling property with a purchase option is a great way to profit while helping complete the dream of home ownership for others. Much of the best property is located in the older industrial cities of the Mid-Atlantic to Midwest (Western Pennsylvania to Minnesota) and the Mid-South region (Virginia to South Carolina). Smaller towns may have good housing stock but an insufficient number of buyers to make this concept work.

You want to look for properties, preferably single-family homes, that have at least three bedrooms. This investment is not the type that calls for a complete rehab, but all of the cosmetic work (painting, carpeting, cabinets, and so on) needs to be completed before the house is put on the market. Sometimes, a really well-valued property that only needs a touch-up may be appealing enough, and you can offer your future buyer a chance to pick out colors. Your customer needs to be able to see themselves staying for many years in this house.

Your total investment in this property should be no more than 70 percent of the appraised value, after the work has been completed. Keep the total price of the project at a level that your buyer will have as little difficulty as possible qualifying for a mortgage. You can easily estimate what a low to moderate income can qualify for, as well as afford. While interest rates continue to remain on the low side, rent-to-own is a great way to solve a housing problem. A buyer's mortgage payments will likely end up being less than the current rent. What's more, you are creating additional stability to the community by increasing home ownership.

SET THE SALE PRICE

The price will be established at the time the buyer signs the lease option, even though the buyer is renting the property at the moment. The option portion of the lease will include that price as well as the term of the option. If the deal closes in that term (usually in a year), that price will hold; if the period stretches longer, the price will have to be renegotiated.

You should handle the details of this transaction as if it is a stand-alone rental. Make sure that you have positive cash flow from the rental payments. Taking a break-even deal because you are looking for the profits from the sale of the property may be very shortsighted. Remember that some deals never close. Future profits are always a speculative consideration.

PRESCREEN YOUR TENANT/OWNERS

You are looking for potential owners, not just renters, so you will need to spend more time making sure that even if your candidate isn't eligible now, you both know what it will take to get a mortgage. Have your candidate fill out a loan application and submit it to a banker or a mortgage broker who will work with them. You both need to know where the problem areas are and create a plan together to correct them.

If you are working with clients with little verifiable income information, they should be made aware that virtually every mortgage company requires some stability in income. Some people make a major portion of their money off the books to avoid tax payments. However, if they want to own a home, they will have to secure and keep a steady on-the-record job. Perhaps understanding the tax deduction benefits of owning a home would soften the blow. Part of your role is to educate.

Once you have been involved in the real estate business for any length of time, you will become familiar with credit scores and where an applicant has to be for a mortgage approval. The range of scores runs from approximately 350 to 850. Under 550 and financing is extremely difficult if not impossible. Over 650 and it is fairly easy. Explain the elements of this score and how it can be raised.

A low credit score, as discussed in Chapter 3, can be the result of having previous credit problems such as collections or charge-offs (debts that are written off because they are uncollectible). Work history and residence history also add or subtract from the score. Some additional elements are the total amount of outstanding credit and particularly how high it is in relation to income, and the length of time that any credit has been in place. A large amount of recent credit will subtract from the total score. The process of credit scoring is a complicated mathematical formula not easily understood, but a series of good practices will improve a poor or borderline score. You need to help your customer get to this point.

USE THE SERVICES OF A CREDIT RESTORATION COMPANY

Professionals in most cities can work with people who have blemishes on their credit report and cause them to be removed or improved. If you are going to sell any quantity of property under rent-to-own programs, you need to join forces with such a service. Be careful about the specific company you use because some charge a high fee and do not work with clients closely enough. You are looking for a good, effective service, not any referral fees. Your profit will come from a successful transaction.

The ways to improve a credit score range from paying off old debts to challenging negative information. A creditor must respond within a specific period to any dispute that is raised, and some will remove the negative comments rather than research them. An efficient restoration program can improve a score fifty to one hundred points in six months with the cooperation of the client. That may be all it takes to get a mortgage.

COMMUNICATE REGULARLY WITH YOUR BUYER

You've made the sale, but it doesn't count until it closes. This type of transaction takes some ongoing attention. Keep in touch with your buyers to see if they are still happy with the house and on track with their mortgage process. They may have questions or they may need encouragement. You need to provide answers and support. You also should be in touch with the mortgage broker to make sure all documentation is being submitted as requested. The margins on these deals are good, but work is involved. Hand-holding is important.

YOU ARE RESPONSIBLE FOR MAINTENANCE

You may have made a future sale, but for the present you have only a rental agreement. This is different from an installment sale under a land contract, where title passes to the new owner. Your customer is only a tenant for the time being, so you will continue to have all of the maintenance responsibilities to perform. The last thing you want is for the sale to fall through, so the condition of the property is very important. Your "buyer" may walk away from the down payment if he or she is no longer enthusiastic about the purchase or discovers that major repairs are soon to come. You definitely do not want a property returned that needs major work to resell or rent again.

TRACK ALL MONIES CAREFULLY

You will be receiving a cash down payment of a mutually agreed-to amount when your rent-to-own client becomes your tenant. Although this money is defined a nonrefundable deposit, you need to track it as well as any other payment credits you may be offering. Some sellers will offer a $100/month allocation towards closing costs if all of the rent is paid timely. This incentive increases the likelihood that the property will close. Your deal should be profitable enough to allow you to make such accommodations. Remember that you bought the property at a discounted price, and you are selling it at full retail.

ARRANGE THE CLOSING

These tenants are on a one-year lease that should end by then or even before with the completion of the purchase. In six to eight months, you should be able to see the progress required to secure a mortgage for the purchase price. If everything is on track, you should then set a target date for closing.

If little progress has been made or perhaps even new problems such as unemployment create even more questions about your tenants' securing a mortgage, you will have to make some decisions. You need to put everything in writing.

You could decide that the lease term is over after this one year and will not be renewed and that the option has expired. You could extend the deal for a short period of time. You could, if you wanted, renegotiate the entire deal, including the purchase price. By now, you should know your tenant/buyer well enough to be able to predict if a little extra time will actually help or not. The one thing you should not do is to ignore the situation, as you may end up with a major problem on your hands. If you had planned on getting your equity out from a sale, the house needs to go back on the market again.

AFTER THE DEAL CLOSES

Most folks who make a home purchase through a rent-to-own deal are thrilled once the deal is complete and they actually own the home. Remember to ask for referrals, as they are the best advertising you can get. Proud new homeowners will tell everyone they know. New candidates will seek you out.

This type of transaction may take more time and more hand-holding than others, but a rent-to-own can be the most satisfying as well. In most deals, you are buying at wholesale, selling at retail, and making a good profit over the short term. You're also helping someone realize the dream of home ownership. A great deal for all!

CHAPTER

ONE MAN'S MISERY

WADE'S STORY

The dream of every investor is to find a property that has been foreclosed on and then to be able to purchase it for pennies on the dollar. In recent years, mortgages have been easier to get and a number of families have taken on large second mortgages as well, to finance cars and vacations. Added to a sluggish economy, you have all the conditions for a substantial rise in the number of foreclosures. On the other hand, with more investors in the market, they are, in some cases, bidding up the prices of these distressed sales, so the bargains are tougher to find.

My own first experience with a foreclosure was as good as it gets. It started with a call from the president of the small savings and loan that financed one of my earliest deals, asking me if I might be interested in a duplex that the bank had foreclosed on. I always answer these questions positively, because I want the chance to bid on anything that might be of interest. No bidding was necessary here, though, because the deal they were offering was to pay off the old mortgage with a new note and required no money down. It sounded too good to be true, but in this case, it wasn't.

The property was a side-by-side duplex with two bedrooms in each unit located in a solid Pittsburgh neighborhood. The units were in good condition, and tenants were living happily in both spaces. Instant cash flow! This seemed like a deal only experts could come across, and here I was—new to the business.

I immediately went back to the bank to start the paperwork. Curious, I asked the president why he would do something like this for me. He explained that when they have to foreclose on a property, the main concern of his board of trustees is that the property begin generating cash flow again. They weren't concerned with the price as long as they didn't lose any money. So, someone else had been paying off a mortgage and now I would realize the profit. The deal closed in less than a month.

This is one of the best ways to locate foreclosures: develop a relationship with a bank and let them know you are looking for properties. My current headquarters building came directly from the bank on a foreclosure, and they financed it completely as well. You must learn to stay in contact with any banks you use on a constant basis, although this only works with smaller community or regional banks. Drop in from time to time to make your payments or do general banking. Find out who is in charge of foreclosures and ask if they have anything new on the books. You just might show up at the right time.

The larger banks have a more formalized procedure that begins the minute a mortgage goes into default. Foreclosures are often handled by in-house legal teams, and when the process is over, they contact a real estate company to put it on the Multiple Listing Service (MLS) list. The price is not set at a bargain rate, and it is likely to take a while for the price to come down, if it ever does. Many larger banks simply hold the property until they get close to their price.

Over the years, I have bought a substantial number of foreclosures, most of them directly from the bank after all the proceedings are complete. But I have also made some good deals with a borrower either going into default or already there. These deals can be terrific bargains, but they are far more complex. They sell to me "subject to" their current liens, and I negotiate with the lenders or creditors.

While any investor should learn the basics of buying foreclosures, you should approach them very cautiously. Keep an eye out for an easy one to come along, but unless you have a law degree or some good financial services experience, don't get too involved until you know all of the rules. Always consult a professional for advice.

TWO TYPES OF FORECLOSURES

The first thing to learn about is the two different types of housing finance instruments that are used in different states. One is a traditional mortgage that most of us may feel we understand, and the other is called a Trust Deed. To simplify the explanation, the first is a direct transaction between the lender and the borrower. The second is actually a three-party transaction with the addition of a trustee who has legal standing to protect the lender's interest until the property is paid off. Unless the loan goes into default, both finance instruments will look very much the same.

The foreclosure procedure on both of these types of financial instruments are five stages long, beginning with a default (ninety days in arrears in payments) and ending with the property reverting back to the lender. In a Trust Deed situation, the proceedings are conducted by a trustee without any additional court involvement. With a mortgage, the formal action of a court is required before the sheriff can conduct the property auction.

During the final stage of some of these proceedings (and only in some states), the borrower has a chance to redeem the property by paying off what is due. Most states that use Trust Deeds do not have this period, but many mortgage states do. Remember, a loan in default triggers the clause that makes the entire amount due. So, a $100,000 loan that went into default with $5,000 of missed payments now costs the full $100,000 *plus* expenses to redeem. Consider this if you are dealing with a seller whose loan is already in the default stage.

SEVERAL WAYS TO PLAY

At least three ways, and perhaps even a fourth way, are possible to acquire a property in foreclosure. The methods take different skills and require differing amounts of money. Some require cash and negotiation skills, and others are merely formal transactions. You should explore all of the ways to acquire property including attending the auction—although this approach is the most difficult. Your options are:

1. Before the sale takes place.
2. During the sale.
3. During the redemption period.
4. After the foreclosure is completed.

THE PREFORECLOSURE DEAL

Once a loan is about to go into default, everyone, including the property owner, knows how it will likely end up. The property will go up for sale and the borrower will lose his or her equity, credit rating, and perhaps even more. You may be the answer to the problem.

You are very likely to hear from these delinquent owners as a result of your aggressive "We Buy Houses" cards and ads. They know that they are in trouble, even if they aren't sure how to get out of it. If the property has equity (the sale value is in excess of the existing

loan), you may even be able to hand them some money in the transaction and take over the amount of their existing mortgage. Many
lenders would be willing to rewrite the loan to a new investor who
will be able to pay. Your only cash needs may be what you pay to the
seller, plus any legal fees.

At times, however, the mortgage amount is higher than the value
of the property. Your negotiating skills come into play in these situations. You can make a tentative agreement with the owner "subject to
financing," and then go to the bank and see if you can settle the debt
for a lesser amount. Lenders are astute enough to understand the situation and how much the property is really worth, and some are willing to make a deal to settle at a discount without going through the
time and the expense of a foreclosure. The larger the bank, however,
the more formalized the negotiations and the more difficult to get an
agreement.

BUYING AT AUCTION

Auctions present a number of real challenges for any beginning investor. First, you are unlikely to be able to make an inspection of the
property before it is sold at auction. Most homeowners in a foreclosure situation are having general financial problems, and you can almost assume that much of the general maintenance has been
neglected. Plan on a budget for that work in addition to the purchase
price. Is it still a bargain?

You will not receive a seller's disclosure of the homes sold at auction, and you will buy it on an as-is basis. Major roof, electrical, or
plumbing problems may exist, and those problems become yours.

You will need cash for this type of deal, so any financing you require will have to be in place before the sale begins. Because you do
not know exactly what the house will be worth, you may not be able
to borrow against the equity until much later in the game. No mortgage contingencies here.

Still enthusiastic? Consider that you may have to evict the current owner or tenant, because many people do not leave their property during these proceedings. They're hoping that they can avoid foreclosure at the last minute. You will own the property as the result of the auction, but you may still have to secure possession through eviction proceedings. These can take time—as long as months and years—and cost money. You will be paying an attorney to do research and attend the sale. Then you have the cost of the sheriff or the court as well.

However, these auction transactions still have a major upside potential; the price is based on the mortgage balance, not on the market price. Therefore, a home that is worth $200,000 with a defaulted $50,000 mortgage will go up for sale at the lower number, which is the unpaid loan. Without much active bidding, you may find yourself with quite a bargain.

But you want to determine whether the foreclosure action was initiated by the first or the second mortgage holder, because there is a substantial difference. If the default is on the first, all other mortgages will fall off after the sale, and the lender will have recourse *only* against the borrower. If the default is on a second or even third mortgage, the sale is subject to the liens on more senior mortgages. You are buying out one loan, but you will still have to pay out the others. Have a lawyer or a title company do a search for you before you make any bids. In fact, you may want to work closely with an attorney at least when you are a beginner at foreclosures.

THE REDEMPTION PERIOD

In some states (not all) where mortgages are the lending instrument, a period exists after the auction when the defaulted borrower can redeem the property by paying off the loan—perhaps ninety days or beyond. For auction buyers, this period is when they are waiting to finalize the sale and evict the occupant, whether it's the tenant or owner.

If there is equity in the property and the owner can't pay off the loan, you, as an investor, may be able to buy the rights to do so and then step in and take over the property by paying off the mortgage in default. While this transaction may be very profitable in certain situations, you will need professional legal advice as many sellers in this situation don't really understand their rights.

ALL WORK AND NO PAY

Becoming a foreclosure player may be a complicated way to invest in real estate. You must begin by learning as much as you can about the process. Then before you make a bid on a specific property, you have to do your homework. Determine the general value of the property and then make an on-site inspection. If you can get in, you'll want to do that. Then find out about the mortgages to make sure which one you are bidding on. Be prepared that, at the end of the day, after you have done the legwork, you may not be the high bidder. Others may take the numbers higher than you think will work. Some auctions attract a lot of attention while others attract little.

BUYING AFTER THE FORECLOSURE IS OVER

If there are no bids at an auction, the lienholder who put up the property will claim possession of it. That could range from a private money lender to a bank to a government agency such as the Small Business Administration (SBA) (when the property secured a business loan to the Veterans Administration [VA] or HUD, which may have guaranteed the loan). Each situation will be handled in a slightly different way, but there are opportunities in each.

The government will post a list of their foreclosed properties in papers and on websites. You will know the amount required, and the listing will tell you exactly how to go about submitting your offer.

A number of government agencies deal with mortgages or have the ability to foreclose on defaulted loans, the largest being HUD—

the department of Housing and Urban Development. These agencies back Federal Housing Administration (FHA) loans. These types of loans offer guarantees to banks that make them more likely to issue mortgages with lower down payments. Defaults are covered by the government guarantee and go into their inventory to be sold.

Another government-backed mortgage program is under the Veterans Administration, which will pay off defaults and sell off property. Many of these properties are sold through real estate brokers.

Homes or rental property are sometimes used to secure business loans. If they are free of individual mortgages, the SBA may be selling them to liquidate a defaulted loan.

Finally, some properties are sold by bankruptcy trustees to meet debtor obligations. A sale may be made by the trustee, but it will be available to a higher bidder in open court. The U.S. Bankruptcy Court in your district can give you a list of the panel of trustees, and you can contact them to tell them of your interest in these sales.

Other agencies have websites where information is posted. Any good search engine can provide all of the Internet addresses you will need.

A bank's handling of what are referred to as REOs (Real Estate Owned) will vary depending on the size of the bank. Smaller institutions may offer their property to sale to the first person who asks or to good customers who are known to be real estate investors. The bank wants to put the loan back on their books as a performing loan as quickly as possible, so the first reasonable offer usually gets the deal.

Larger banks have established departments and procedures to handle their foreclosure property. They are in a better position to hold the property for a longer time and want to maximize the sale price so that they cover not only the outstanding loan but the cost of the process itself. They are more likely to list their properties with a real estate firm and to sell them at a price far closer to retail than you might think.

Private lenders (the hard-money lenders we described earlier) may be another hidden but excellent source for investing in foreclosure property. First, such lenders seldom have a loan that is over 60 percent of the property value. Second, they are normally busy making loans and have few structures to sell off the ones they take back; third, they do some aggressive write-offs to offset profits. You may really find a deal here.

The caution here is that most of the property is in rehab and often is not finished at the time it is taken back. You may have a serious construction project on your hands, but if you buy right, you should have enough money to cover it.

LET THE GAMES BEGIN

The foreclosure process is like a large chess game. You will deal with the financial and legal systems at work and then play against other investors who want to win as well. Learn all the rules before you start. Also, don't get too caught up in the action, which might prevent you from making the only moves that benefit you.

LOCATING THE HIDDEN SELLER

now be a motivated seller. My first success was a three-unit building that looked interesting, but I thought it to be overpriced.

The first time I talked to the seller, he wasn't very anxious, but all that had changed six weeks later when the property still hadn't been sold. My second call had a much stronger reception, and I learned the price had been dropped by $20,000. Then he offered to pay some of my closing costs, which convinced me. The cash flow was now easily positive, and I bought the building.

I have made it a habit to check back on properties that I think would be interesting, even if they are overpriced. Owners may not be motivated in the beginning, but if they haven't made the sale happen in a few months, they may be very ready to deal. Be persistent but not pushy.

My goal is always to locate the hidden seller and make the best possible deals with them. (A hidden seller is an owner who has not listed or advertised the property but would like to sell.) I want to stay away from where other investors will gather so I don't get into bidding wars. I am very competitive and might be tempted into overpaying because I don't like to lose.

I have business cards that are printed with the slogan "We Buy Houses," and I circulate them as much as I can. I give at least five to everyone who will take them. I know that some will get thrown away, but some will end up in the hands of motivated sellers, and the printing costs are pennies compared to the return. In fact, one morning, I had a call from a woman who was concerned about a piece of property an hour away from my area. It had been her mother's home, and the family needed to sell it immediately. Not until the closing did I find out she got my name from a card she found "on the floor of a car dealer." I have no idea how it got there.

I use my business cards as much as possible and mail out marketing postcards on a regular basis. I know there are times my name gets in front of a seller at almost the same time they begin thinking about selling. I really welcome those calls. If I carefully explore their problems and make an offer that solves them, we can both walk away satisfied. The key is to ask the right questions and to find out how much cash they need from the sale. I am talking about money in their pocket after everything else is paid. These hidden sellers believe they need to get out from a property they own, and if I make it easy enough for them, they will.

Advertising is a good idea for any business, and I always put ads in the paper looking for houses for sale. More powerful than that, I pay referral fees to people who send interested sellers to me. My best success has been with people who work around houses in a neighborhood on a regular basis, such as contractors, meter readers, postal delivery people, and even my tenants in other properties. When they find out that a property may be going up for sale, they call me. If I make the deal, I give them a finder's fee of $250. This is easy money for them and certainly worth it to me.

To this day, I receive calls from people who made a referral to me years ago. They often ask if I am still looking for property. I know they are really asking if I still pay a fee. Of course I do. Where else could I get a small army scouting for me who act as my eyes and ears in the market?

Business cycles go up and down. There are times when cars and clothing are selling well and others when they are not. It may be a function of the time of year or the general economy. Property, on the other hand, is always coming on the market, but real estate activity still reflects the times. In a flourishing economy, owners are selling to move up. When times are tough, owners are selling to save money.

Growing families need more space, whereas empty nesters need less. Some investors are building portfolios, and others are liquidating theirs. The good news about these cycles is that there will always be a supply to choose from, and some of the deals will be very profitable for you. You need to know as quickly as you can about any properties that are about to become available. Being first on the scene will often give you an advantage. Some investors come back when no one else is interested.

We've already discussed distressed properties and their advantages as well as possibilities for complications. These properties are on a continual flow into the market, but many other investors may be following them as well. Competition may mean higher prices.

You will find the hidden markets in houses and buildings not yet listed, a forgotten listing, or even ones that are not quite yet put on the market for sale privately. Owners think about getting out for a variety of reasons.

You can find the forgotten listing by monitoring the paper and checking back with owners that you may have had contact with in the past. They may be ready to drop the price or provide credit for closing costs or do some creative financing as a way to move the property. If you find a property just coming out of an agent's listing term, the price should drop, at least by the commission amount, right away.

Your cards and postcards will put your name and number in front of people who may be on the verge of selling their home or knowing someone who is. You might even create a door hanger with your message on it and pay some teenagers to blanket a neighborhood with them. Just make sure that you impress on your helpers that you don't want them strewn around or placed where they shouldn't be. You are making an impression about your reliability, and you want the impression to be the right one.

Referral fees are also very effective tools, but make sure that you manage the program with a good level of organization and that you record the information on both the property and who gave you the information. You will need to pay these fees promptly, and if you plan to deduct the fees as a cost, you will have to issue a tax document called a 1099, which covers such commissions. When finding property for wholesaling, some investors use bird-dogs—a preselected group of folks who pay to join, get some training in what to look for, and split profits on deals they find. An investor who works with this type of group virtually always wins in the long run, and the finder has a chance to earn money while learning the ropes.

You might want to specialize in areas or neighborhoods that others don't frequent. The inner city can be a tough place, but just a few streets away may be some stable housing good for purchasing Section 8 rentals or even selling on a rent-to-own. Become a familiar face in the area and get to know the residents. They will remember to call you when something might be coming up for sale or when someone is looking to rent or to buy. People tend to stay close to areas that are familiar to them, so referrals bring tenants and buyers as well.

A house just going up for sale does not have a firm price, particularly in the lower price ranges. In many areas, properties priced below $100,000 (and perhaps even higher in some places) are rarely listed by real estate agents. The commissions, after all the expense and the splits, do not justify it. One of the real values of having an agent is that they help an owner to determine the price of their property by comparing it to others in the area. Without this help, new sellers and particularly motivated sellers use a different criteria to set a price. They are more concerned about what they need to settle debts, find a new place to live, or put some money away for safety. You need to learn as much about pricing and the buyer's circumstances as you can. Create a list of questions to ask, and be diligent about doing so every time you interview someone who has contacted you looking to sell their property.

You may be able to give them a little cash and take over a mortgage, or you may be able to finance a first mortgage to give them the cash they need and have them hold a second that pays out over a period of time. If you listen closely to what your seller tells you, you can make a deal that gives both of you what you need.

Older neighborhoods provide some interesting opportunities. Sellers who have lived in their homes for many years have likely paid far less than the current market value. Housing prices with very few exceptions have gone up year after year. Their loans were taken out on these lower amounts, and they have been paying on them for years so balances are small. Some houses have second and even third mortgages that have been taken out to pay off old debt or finance some new expenditure. There are homes that have more debt than equity.

You will benefit yourself in the long run by focusing on some specific geographical areas, working hard to become known, and creating a group of satisfied customers. They will prove a good source of referrals and recommendations.

CHAPTER 11

GOING FOR BROKE

WADE'S STORY

From my first job as a teenager to the last corporate job I held, my goal has been to work for myself. I don't like reporting to someone else; I don't mind working hard, but I want to set my own hours and I like to follow my instincts, not a company's rules. I want to be free. I welcome the risk even when things get tough.

My first real estate purchase generated a positive cash flow of $200 a month. With a few more purchases in not too much time, that exceeded $1,000 a month. My gas company job netted me about $2,500 a month, so it seemed logical that once I reached that magical number, I could go on my own. There were a few things that I didn't consider.

My parents, proud of my efforts, pitched in to help. My mother was keeping my books, and my dad was doing most of the minor repairs on my properties. All of this was for free. They had retired from their full-time jobs, and they were very loyal and reliable! I was on my way out of corporate life, starting two companies, Houses Unlimited, Inc., and Affordable Properties. I just knew I was on the road to my first million.

I can still remember that look on my boss's face when I handed in my resignation. I had a nice job with good prospects, and he told me, understandably, that people didn't walk away from jobs like that. He offered to hold my letter in his desk for a few days and not mention it to anyone while I thought about it, but I insisted he accept it then. I didn't want a safety net to fall back on.

It didn't take me long to realize that rental cash flow is nice until you have to live off of it. It doesn't all stay in your pocket. One answer was to buy more rentals, but that wasn't quite as easy as I had expected. Every purchase added expense, so soon I had to hire real paid employees to help handle the work load, which increased my costs even more. Now, too, I was paying benefits instead of receiving them. But I was happy being self-employed and determined to make it succeed.

My first solution to my cash problems was not a good one. I began to refinance my properties, taking out the cash and using it to pay bills. I had purchased many of the properties at good prices, so additional equity was available. I wasn't considering, however, that the new debt would come along with higher payments, which then decreased my positive cash flow.

This was all happening about the time that I began to wholesale properties, and the profits caused my cash flow to grow. Eventually it began to even out and I wasn't cashing in equity; I was back to building it.

One other challenge that I didn't take into consideration when becoming a full-time investor was that it would be harder to obtain some loans because I no longer had steady income from a job. The smaller banks I did have a relationship with continued to work with me, but new ones wanted to see a track record of my business, which was too new.

I remember the words of my college coach: "It's not what you can do that gets you ahead, it's what you can't do that holds

you back." In the beginning, running a business was not a skill I
had developed, but I have learned how critical it is.

Starting a full-time real estate business is the same as starting any
other type of business. While it may take little or no cash to begin
purchasing properties, being in business for yourself does take capital. You have to consider not just yourself but others you're dealing
with regularly

You will need to meet the needs of your growing number of tenants: handling their money, paperwork, inquiries, and maintenance
and repairs. You will need to meet the needs of your buyers and sellers by completing transactions on time and smoothly. You will need
to meet the needs of your lenders by making payments on time and
generating financial records on a regular basis. You will need a group
of professionals—lawyers and accountants—and they will require you
to produce records for their review. Professional fees could be high at
times. This will all take time and money, and if you aren't prepared or
run short, the results can be the loss of the property you currently
own.

One of the real challenges of a real estate investment company is
finding the right source of capital. Many business start-ups are financed with a combination of owner equity and borrowed funds. For
people who have been purchasing property, they have likely borrowed
a substantial amount of money already. Finding new cash sources to
create and staff the infrastructure of a business is going to be far more
difficult than the secured borrowing of real estate purchases. Raising
money by cashing in equity and increasing mortgage loans is risky because this adds to payments and decreases positive cash flow at a time
when you need the extra cash to pay overhead.

The primary overhead in the beginning will be the cost of *you*.
Giving up your regular job means that you have to replace your salary
as well as cover the cost of your benefits. You can cut back on personal
expenses for a short while, but this can't go on for long; nor would you

want it to. The worst way to finance this cost is to borrow against credit cards or use them to pay living expenses. Interest rates may be very high, and your monthly cash needs will increase as these bills come due. Such borrowing also has a negative effect on your personal credit that may keep you from being able to borrow additional investment funds. Once you start on this cycle, getting off is not quite so easy.

TIME FOR A BUSINESS PLAN

Every successful enterprise begins with a well-conceived written business plan. This approach may not be necessary when you are a casual or part-time investor, but once you have made the choice to make it your primary pursuit, it is critical. A written business plan will not only help you learn very important information about the cash management side of your business; it will require you to think through a future strategy. You'll have a number of different directions in which to go, and now is the time to decide which ones meet your future goals. How long do you expect to be active in the business? Are you building a portfolio of rental property to provide for an early retirement? Is the thought of being a landlord for the next decade more than you can stand, and are you looking to cash out? Putting it down on paper will help you think it through. Most new business owners cringe at the thought of creating this document, but it is necessary and you can get help. Contact the Small Business Development Center at your local university, which might offer classes as well as free consultants to help you work through the process. You can also read books written for new business owners.*

*Suzanne Caplan, *Streetwise Finance and Accounting* (Adams Media, 2000); Suzanne Caplan and Alan Cech, *Streetwise Small Business Success Kit* (Adams Media, 2002); Rita Lesonsky, *Start Your Own Business* (Entrepreneur Media, 2001); Jan King, *Business Plans to Game Plans* (Wiley, 2003); Courtney Price, *Small Business Answer Kit: 101 Solutions to Survive and Thrive* (Wiley, 2003).

UNDERSTANDING A PRO-FORMA STATEMENT

There are different ways to project future cash flow in a business, and they are far more accurate if they are done carefully. You will find a number of computer-generated formats you can use by simply entering estimated numbers and an estimated percentage of change. However, the point here is not just to produce a theoretical document simply to have one, but to think through each number carefully so you will know how much cash is available to cover expenses and how much may be available for future investing. You will be able to determine when and how much salary you can draw and at what point you can hire others to take care of some of the administrative tasks. As you buy and sell and hold property, much about your financial performance will change. You can't always predict what will be on the market in the future, but you can set goal numbers and change them as necessary. You may have to work harder or differently to achieve what you need.

A profit and loss statement and a cash flow statement are very different, and this difference is even more pronounced in a real estate business. Profit is what is left after all expenses are covered, but in real estate profit includes depreciation which, though substantial, is a noncash item. On the other hand, your expense does not include payments made to principal, so a business can show a loss yet have positive cash flow. This is one of the tax benefits of real estate, which is discussed elsewhere in this book. Property depreciation shelters income from taxes but seemingly has no actual out-of-pocket expense. Remember, however, this is a tax allowance to account for the aging of the property and the wear that accompanies that aging. This *will* have a cost over the years, so you will need to make allowances for repairs and maintenance. In any given year, your expenses may be higher or lower than the depreciation allowance. The actual cash expense becomes a line item in your cash flow statement. There will be few years when you won't have some expenditure.

CASH FLOW INCLUDES PAYMENTS OF PRINCIPAL

A cash flow statement accounts for all forms of cash revenue, including proceeds from loans. The cash outflow does not include depreciation but does include the principal portion of any loan. These payments increase the amount of cash going back to lenders and affect the money you have to operate the business. You should also include any balloon payments, any planned maintenance work, and any seasonal increases in utilities and tax payments due. You may be surprised at the number of months you will have deficit cash. Knowing in advance helps you to plan for them. Always keep some cash in reserve; you will be able to make better decisions this way.

A Cash Flow Statement includes the following:

Starting Cash (all of your available proceeds from loan, sales and rentals)

Plus all collections and new borrowings

Total Available Cash

Less all expense of operations and repairs

Less all loan payments (principal AND interest)

Remaining Cash Balance (or deficit) which is carried over to the next period.

HOW MUCH REVENUE DO YOU NEED?

You need sufficient income from all of your real estate activities to fund all of the direct costs (loan interest, taxes, utilities, and so on) and all of the fixed costs, which include your salary and the expense of any other employees or professionals you may need to use, and your office expense as well as vehicles. Phones, answering service, and computer equipment are all fixed expenses. They stay the same regardless of your activity.

If you are engaging in a variety of activities such as rental income and wholesaling, be sure to account for the month-to-month changes in each type of revenue. There will be vacancies from time to time, and sales and closings will be better some months than others. Use a conservative estimate; it is always better to have more cash than less. Create a budget for expenses based on projected income.

THE RIGHT MOVES AT THE RIGHT TIME

The part-time, casual real estate investor may actually make more money than the early-stage full-time player. A common mistake is underestimating the amount of overhead required to support a large number of rental properties or to record a substantial number of transactions. The active landlord will spend time showing available units, collecting rent, keeping leases up to date, and handling maintenance requests. There may not be much time to find the deals you want and need. That lack of time is often what will drive you to hire someone.

The record-keeping side—tracking income and paying all bills once they have been verified—is extensive as well. Properties that are bought and sold must have settlement sheets recorded, and work is involved in preparing for a closing. The tricky strategy is growing as large as you can while keeping your other employment, and then expanding your interests quickly but carefully after making the transition to a full-time real estate business.

Making wholesale purchases of properties (a substantial number in one transaction) may seem like a good choice, but one that should be scrutinized. A single property, bought because of its potential to be fixed up easily and rented or upgraded to charge higher rents, may not hurt you if it turns out to underperform. But a group of properties, all needing attention at the same time, could drain human as well as financial resources quickly and put everything at jeopardy. If you are thinking of a move like this, be sure you look at each property individually. One or two problems can be handled; more than that should be avoided. Resist the urge if you have any questions.

Back to the business plan: Understand that lean times will happen and plan for them in advance. Every business has a start-up phase, and while you may think you can avoid this because of your previous part-time status, chances are you will go through some if not all aspects of it. Remember, even when the cash is short, you are making profits you can't see—in the appreciation of your holdings. You are building equity that will eventually pay off.

GETTING ON THE RIGHT PATH

One of the interesting aspects of real estate investment is the variety of ways to make money. While buying rental property, you may come across interesting rehabs. While renting your units, you will meet tenants who aspire to ownership. You actually may end up in a variation of the business that you didn't expect. Be open to the possibilities, and you raise your chance of great success. But write a business plan, set business goals, know what it will take to reach them, and understand that what you're doing is a business and not a full-time hobby.

CHAPTER

FINDING QUALIFIED CONTRACTORS

WADE'S STORY

In the process of rehabbing a six-unit building I had recently purchased, I realized that one of the major elements would be the replacement of six separate heating units. I knew it was going to be a major expense, so I called several contractors. The first bid in was from someone I had used previously, but it was higher than I had expected or budgeted. I was hoping that I could get some other quotes and that one might be lower. That's when I ran into a guy I knew from my hometown, who told me that he just started his own heating and cooling company. *What perfect timing*, I thought to myself, *he was starting out, and I could give him some help*. The bid was surprisingly low, half of the original one I had, and that should have sent up a red flag. But I was too new to see it and too anxious to help out someone else.

My new contractor showed up exactly when he said he would, and I gave him 33 percent down on the first furnace, so he would be able to purchase his supplies. I know what it's like when you're just starting out and don't have much cash. Our agreement was that each furnace would be paid for once the installation was complete. Even with that fairly liberal policy, my old friend was calling me almost every day, asking for another advance to make yet another purchase of supplies. I had allowed this relationship to become too friendly and not professional, and he felt as if he could use me like his personal automatic teller machine. Worse yet, I was allowing it.

I was relieved when he finished his work on time and the job was done. I had saved money, even if he was a pain. It was the middle of summer, but I tested the furnaces and they seemed to work great. Unfortunately, as soon as the first cold nights hit in the fall, I had six calls, one from each tenant complaining that they had no heat. I tried but could not make any contact with my old friend. No one answered his phone, not even a voice mail. Not exactly a professional business. He never did call me back. I sent my original heating man, and he went to check things out. All six furnaces had been improperly installed and needed to be reinstalled. Added to what I had already paid, the cost grew much higher than my regular contractor had estimated in the first place. I should have known better.

I've had other tough experiences with contractors, and sometimes I still don't see it coming. I've hired some who seemed entirely professional, drove new trucks, gave written estimates, and employed a steady crew. Their prices aren't usually the lowest, but when time is critical, price isn't my only consideration. Some have performed well, but one in particular didn't finish the job for almost six months when he promised thirty days. I had given him 50 percent of the fee for the job up front (which is often required), and it took the threat of a lawsuit to get the job completed.

You want to be careful when choosing a contractor. You may be new at the business, but you want to find others who are experienced. Check their references and perhaps even visit some of their job sites. Don't become their banker, and don't get involved in their personal problems. When you find contractors who are particularly good, hang on to them and treat them right. You'll be glad to have them available when needed.

A good property manager may have ongoing ties with a number of contractors and be able to refer a lot of business to them, so they put these jobs on a priority. That's the type of relationship I have with my contractors, and I ultimately started my own heating company. Now I understand the problems from the other side, but I try to be extra careful with my investor clients.

KNOW WHAT HAS TO BE DONE

From the beginning, you must decide how much work is to be done and under what budgetary constraints. Every aspect of this type of contract job has a range from the lowest cost to the most luxurious. You can replace worn or stained carpet with industrial-grade rugs or 100 percent wool. New kitchen cabinets and bathrooms can range from the low-cost and very basic to the very ornate. All jobs should have a target budget, and you are the one who needs to set the specifications. Spend some time at the home improvement store and become familiar with the most basic terms.

When you begin to get contractor bids, have in mind how much work you plan to do and at what price point you expect to be. You are going to ask for written bids, but you want to make sure that everyone is bidding on the same scope of work. Your contractors shouldn't be the only ones who know what is to be done. A well-informed customer is one who makes a profit but has as few surprises as possible.

CHOOSE YOUR BIDDING CONTRACTORS

You want to interview each new contractor in person, in your office or at the property, so you know exactly who you are dealing with and so that they learn about you as well. If you are meeting without any referral, mention that you are a steady investor and more work is available after this project if the job comes in professionally, on time, and on budget.

Find out how long they have been in business, and get a list of as many previous clients as you can. Verify as much information as you can. You can easily obtain a Dun & Bradstreet report, which will give you the history of the company and its principals, as well as a report of their credit. You may be fronting a substantial amount of money, and you want to make sure the people you're doing business with will be around at the end of the job. Any contractor with a poor credit rating may not be able to pay for their supplies or labor to complete the job. Any unfinished work will likely cost more to complete than you think. New contractors on the site will want to go over what has been done before if they are going to certify the finished job.

Check out any required licenses. Some plumbing and electrical jobs require a licensed professional, and a professional who has the certification places value on his own skills. Keeping a license in good standing requires that any complaints or issues have been checked out.

Check with the Better Business Bureau and find out if any complaints have been lodged against the contracting company you are considering. Don't write a company off for one or two complaints. People have misunderstandings, but make sure the issues have been resolved satisfactorily.

Verify the insurance carried by any contractor you are considering. They need to have a workers' compensation policy to provide coverage in case any injuries occur on the job and liability insurance to cover any accidental damage to anybody's property while they are doing their work. If your contractor has no insurance and something happens when they are on your property, you may be held liable. Your own insurance isn't likely to provide this extensive coverage, so you might be in serious difficulty.

NOW ON TO THE BIDDING

You should give your contractor candidates a list of the specific work you want done and any necessary details. Ask them to write in a detailed price for each specific room or job and to include the type of material they expect to use or install. Each task should be a separate line item. Manufacturers' names may be required.

A bid should include a specific completion time such as "three weeks after award." The bid should have financial terms as well, describing how much is required on signing and if any progress or specific material payments are required. Also included is the length of the guarantee of any of the work. You need to be able to compare all aspects of a contractor's bid, not just price.

PUT THE ACTUAL CONTRACT IN WRITING

Many contractors are small and don't have enough staff to put out formal contracts when they do work. You probably do not want to go through that exercise either, but you need to have some signed writing between the two of you so you both are in agreement about the work to be done, the materials, and the completion date. You can put this in the form of a simple letter stating all of the elements of the job, the price and terms agreed to, and an estimated finished date. Leave a space on the bottom of the letter for both of you to sign. Date the letter, and make sure you each have a copy. Your lawyer may recommend a more complex document, but when you are a fairly small investor dealing with smaller contractors, that formality is not always practical. The point here is not to have a document that can be used in a future lawsuit. Most contractor disputes frankly cost more than they are worth to take to court. Your intent is to make sure you both know what is to be done and when.

CONSIDER ESCROWING FUNDS

You're concerned with having the work done properly and timely. At the same time, your contractor is concerned with being paid in full and on time. One way to meet both of these needs is to put the funds in an escrow account, held by a third party and drawn down as various phases of the work are completed. Escrowing funds is a good approach if the job is very big and may also be a part of the terms of a loan if you have borrowed money for a rehab. Many banks or private money lenders will not disburse funds until some completion benchmarks have been met. An experienced contractor will understand this procedure.

VISIT THE JOB REGULARLY

Even if you are not paying progress payments, you need to make periodic inspections of any work you have contracted. The issue is not merely to make sure that warm bodies are on the job; your concerns are really the quality of the work and whether the time-lines are being met. Most contractors have to move crews from day to day. They may be waiting for material or for some subcontractors to finish. Watch the progress of the job. If it seems slow, ask to meet the contractor on the site. He may have a plan that you don't understand, or trouble may really be brewing. Keep on top of it so you can find a solution before it gets out of hand.

CONSIDER AN EARLY BONUS

Each day a rehab is going on, you are giving up some revenue and still incurring some costs. You may be losing rent or some potential buyers. You will be paying interest on a loan, taxes, and at least basic utilities. Because of these factors, consider offering some of what you would otherwise be spending in the form of a bonus to a contractor who finishes early. Money can be a great motivator. On the other hand, you may even be able to build into your agreement a penalty for a job not being completed within a certain established time frame. These monies would be deducted from the final price.

DO AN INSPECTION AND GET A SIGN-OFF

Once a job is complete, you and your contractor need to inspect all of the work together. If any appliances, furnaces, or other equipment has been installed, make sure you try it out for a complete cycle. Take care that you have been given all of the warranty cards and all of the manuals. You should both sign a sheet certifying that the work is complete and that payment has been made in full.

Finding reliable contractors is very critical to a real estate investor's success. You will increase your odds of having the best contractors available when needed by working with them professionally and paying them promptly.

CHAPTER 13

APPRAISERS, AGENTS, AND OTHER PROFESSIONALS

WADE'S STORY

I assumed that my job would be to make the deals, and everything else would fall into place. I found out that I was wrong when I was retailing a properly I had rehabbed and I had a buyer ready, willing, and able to purchase it for $85,000. I was all set to make a $20,000 profit, which was already spent, in my mind, to pay a few bills and buy another good deal I had just found. No question about my buyer being approved on the mortgage amount, and we were just waiting for the appraisal for the bank. I know that figure can be a subjective number, but I had already run comps so I was confident . . . until this appraisal came in at $70,000—$15,000 less than my price. That's all the bank would lend, and to resolve it, I had to take a second mortgage back from the buyer for the balance. To this day, I believe that house was worth $85,000, and I only recently received my money when the property was refinanced.

Over the years, I have spent hundreds of hours on the

phone with appraisers. Every time, I learn something different. That job is not an easy one, because each new report they do starts with a good bit of research and ends up as an educated guess of what a property is worth. If I ordered ten different appraisals on a property, I am likely to come up with ten different numbers. Some in the business are aggressive and some are very conservative. I try to use the same ones on a regular basis so I can know their tendencies. I never ask them to stretch their appraisals, but I do like the ones who are consistent and fairly middle-of-the-road. There are low comps that can be used, and high ones as well.

The more deals you send to an appraiser, the more information you can get in advance. Not favors, but information. Once you've established a relationship, you can ask for comps in advance or order a drive-by estimate. This simple outside look is not complete enough for any lender, but you will have advance information when you are making a deal.

I work with an entire team of professionals on a regular basis, and some can be quite specialized, having particular knowledge in an area that investors need. You may work with several lawyers, one on general business issues and another on closings and evictions. I tried to handle my first eviction on my own. Although the secretary at the magistrate's office was very helpful, my tenant, who apparently had been through this before, was tricky enough to buy more time in my property without paying for it. I went to my lawyer to review how I was handling things. Now, I may not win them all, but I win most of them. I have a system in place.

I have already talked about the real estate agent I use, Mike Wheeler of Coldwell Banker, who has been a real mentor and friend to me since the very beginning. Most new investors make contact with that kind of agent early in the game. I wasn't aware that I needed a good insurance agent as well. One Saturday, fairly early in my investment career, I found out the importance of a good insurance professional. Luckily, I had someone in place.

I was out running my personal errands when my answering service called. They never bothered me if it wasn't an emergency, and this one really was. One of my properties had caught fire, and I was needed immediately. On my way there, I called my insurance agent, in a panic. She calmed me down and assured me that I was fully covered. In this case, I needed to be, because the damage exceeded $30,000. After a reasonable deductible, the repairs were covered. I had rent-loss protection as well, which paid for my loss of income while the property was being repaired. My agent was careful enough to cover my properties completely, even though I own some of them for less than a year. These transactions often involve a lot of paperwork.

I also spend a good bit of my time at closings, so I work with a good closing company who will do title searches quickly and make sure paperwork is done so the process can go smoothly. In the more complicated cases, I use a lawyer to handle all the details. Some properties have a more confusing history than others, and I need to have title insurance in case of any future questions. In one case, almost three years were needed to get clear title to a property that I could have sold. During that time, I ended up with all of the expense and no income. Not the situation where any investors, new or experienced, want to find themselves.

My sports background taught me a lot about teamwork, and I try to impress the need for a good team of professionals on the new investors I mentor. Business success is now and will always be a team sport.

If you are buying property at the best price in the beginning, you are not likely to be concerned about the appraisals. You should be paying less than 70 percent of the value, so getting the amount of loan you need should not be a problem. For those who do rehabs for resale or sell on a rent-to-own, the appraisal price is critical to your sale closing as well as your profit.

Most of your buyers will finance at least part of their purchase price, which will require having an appraisal sent to the bank or mortgage company. If that number comes in far less than they need, their requested loan amount will as well. You may end up at a closing getting a note instead of cash, which is not what you expect nor want nor likely need. The first step to preventing this conclusion is to learn as much about the appraisal process as you can and find some appraisers to work with on a regular basis. You will find that each lender, whether a bank or a mortgage company, will have a list of approved appraisers. You cannot control this process. Any appearance of trying to do that will make a lender nervous. They may think you are trying to artificially raise the value of the property.

What you want to do is develop your relationship with the lenders and determine who is on their list of approved appraisers. Then get to know them and their tendencies. You will find out who is the most conservative and who is more liberal, and you can gauge the estimated price you might get. Give as much business as you can to a few appraisers, and you both will benefit. You will receive timely service, which may be critical to your cash flow, and you will experience few surprises that you have to compensate for in the financing.

You can learn a good deal from appraisers that will be particularly valuable if you decide to do much property wholesaling. You will be making offers quickly, and the more you learn about valuation, the more astute buyer you will become.

INSURE AGAINST ALL PROBLEMS

New real estate investors may not find it as easy as they expect to get the proper insurance as well as competitive prices. In fact, sometimes getting insurance at all is all but impossible. Many companies do not like to insure properties that are not owner-occupied, and when properties are not occupied at all, insurers see the risks as very high. Kids can play in a vacant house, which can result in damage and even serious fires. Accidental fires may not be found in time when a property is vacant. And a high enough incidence of suspicious fires occurs to create caution among insurers. An agent will have to work at securing insurance for your property. You need to develop a good business relationship with one who will take care of your needs even when the work exceeds the value of their commission on the premium. They are building relationships.

You need to understand that not all deals are profitable for an agent. The insurance coverage on a short-term rehab project is one example. The property is vacant, time is needed to find a carrier, and the coverage may be in effect for less than a year. However, your long-term rental properties will generate premiums year after year without much effort, and the revenues for your agent should equalize over time.

You will not be able to really test out the service of your agent until you have to make your first claim. Then you will see the adequacy of your coverage as well as the ease of filing the paperwork and collecting on your claim. The one thing you can do in advance is to choose an agent who will sit down with you and carefully review all of your needs and what is the most cost-effective coverage. Find an agency that seems really interested in your business.

YOUR BUSINESS ADVISORS

This book covers the needs and choices of lawyers and accountants in a number of different chapters. The purpose is to impress upon the new investor how important it is to choose and then to work with qualified professionals in a variety of areas. Real estate is a complex business, particularly from a legal and accounting standpoint. We will cover the numbers issue in depth a bit later in this book.

Legal questions can get very complicated. You not only need to choose good advisors; you need to use them effectively as well. When you start buying property, you want to have a lawyer look over sales agreements. Some contract exclusions may surprise you after the fact. No one wants to be surprised by taking possession of a property to find that the appliances and lighting fixtures are gone when you thought they might still be there. A competent lawyer looks out for such costly oversights.

Your lawyer will also need to review loan documents, at least in the beginning until you learn all of the standard language. Clauses such as "due on sale" or "cross-collateralization" or "confessions of judgment" are unfamiliar to many nonbanking people, but you need to learn about them. Eventually you will achieve a certain level of comfort.

Beginning as a landlord, you need to have leases and other agreements with tenants looked over for their legality and then consider how you are enforcing them as well. If the time comes to evict a tenant, you are likely to be able to do it yourself, but you may need to get legal advice on some of your process.

Once you begin to sell your property, at the completion of a rehab or as the result of a rent-to-own deal, you will need the services of a closing attorney. The title company can close many deals, but when issues of clear title are involved, a higher level of expertise is likely to be needed. Real estate closings will be a big part of your business work, so make sure you have the best resources in place.

CHAPTER 14

THE CLOSING PROCESS

WADE'S STORY

The details of my first few closings were handled by others. A bank did the first, and my real estate agent took care of the next two. They made it look easy. I just showed up and signed where I was told and walked away as the owner of a property. Now I know the worth of these professionals.

As an investor, I began to orchestrate my own closings, and I had no idea what to do. The first time out, the entire event was delayed for a week because I didn't ask what was required of my seller and me. The title company, knowing that I was an investor, assumed I already knew. These days I hate it when closing is delayed, so I know how everyone else must have felt. For some in the room, occasionally me, it represents needed cash.

I didn't order the title fast enough to allow the title company to do their search on the property, and I even failed to give them the seller's phone number so they could contact him for information. I didn't think to ask for clarification of his marital status, and then I found out he was separated, which meant that his wife would have to sign at the closing. They weren't on the friendliest terms, and for a few days we couldn't locate her. Three days later, she agreed to sign the deed. I hadn't ordered a final water bill, which was from a municipal authority and required in our area, so that the old bill could be paid and the account transferred to a new owner. Basically, I did nothing in advance because I didn't ask any questions. Because I wasn't a regular customer of the title company, they did not go out of their way to help me.

Since that day, I learned to order a title search as soon I place a property under an agreement. If any problems arise, we have time to resolve them. Problems are not uncommon; even the buyer and seller are searched to see if any judgments are pending against them. If there are, they will have to be released or paid at the closing.

Title problems can range from having an old mortgage that has been paid but not recorded as satisfied to all kinds of old debt. One seller owed $10,000 in child support that he would have had to settle at the closing. Added to his mortgage, he would have needed to pay out money to sell his house. He decided it wasn't worth it, and the deal was called off.

One of my most complicated deals happened just recently. A man called to sell me a property owned by his deceased mother. He admitted that they hadn't paid property taxes in the past couple of years, but I told him that would come out in a title search. I made the deal based on his estimate and sold the property the next day to a new investor, coming away with a $5,000 profit. Nice profit on a twenty-four-hour turnaround, I thought.

Turned out there were more than a few problems, though. The mother didn't have an estate, so the son could not just sign over to the buyer. And the unpaid taxes were higher than he thought, and there was no way to give him the $5,000 he was expecting at closing. Once we told him that, he stopped taking my calls. Now the buyer was getting antsy. He was excited about buying real estate, and he loved this deal. I knew he could become a good client, and I didn't want to see this fall apart.

Some investors would walk away. This deal was getting too complicated, but I am too competitive for giving up. I went to the son's house with a notary and a check for $2,500. I was going to close this deal. Part of that money was from my profits, but I figured some profit was better than none—and a happy customer meant more down the road. After I explained to the seller that if he didn't sign, the property would likely go up on a tax sale, he agreed. My check sealed the deal.

No two closings are alike. Some of them actually go fairly smoothly. But buying property from distressed sellers and sometimes selling it to credit-challenged buyers makes for some serious work to make it happen. But that's where the final score is kept, where the money and the property change hands.

A real estate closing is the transaction that conveys a good title in a property from the seller to the buyer. A closing may appear to be a simple chore, but it is at best somewhat complicated and at worst totally confusing. If you are the seller, you want to get paid. If you are the buyer, you want to get a clear title to the property so you can begin to collect rent or rehab for resale. And if you're wholesaling the deal, you won't get paid until this final transaction between your seller and buyer is complete.

The buyer can select who handles the closing transaction. The choice is between a settlement firm or a lawyer who specializes in real estate closings. Difficult deals, such as purchasing from an estate, require a higher level of expertise. The difference in cost between one choice or the other will not be substantial, but if the deal doesn't happen or later issues on the title emerge, the expense can be substantial. Learn as much as you can about the process, and then let a good closing company or lawyer handle it. Make sure you have title insurance to cover any undiscovered mistakes. The title company writes a policy that guarantees good title, or they will pay damages.

The process starts with a title search that identifies the previous owners and transfers on this property. Is the person who has signed the agreement as the seller really legally the property owner? If the property was jointly owned by a couple and one is deceased, the estate should have gone through probate to give the surviving spouse legal right to sell, unless it is titled with the right of survivorship. When the legal owner is incapacitated (in a hospital or nursing home) and an offspring may have power of attorney, that situation still may not give them clear right to transfer title on property. Children who are acting as executors or beneficiaries of a parent's estate must have filed all the proper documents and paid all applicable taxes before selling the real property. The person who appears at the closing to sign over the deed must have clear legal right to do so.

WHAT IS INCLUDED IN THE SALE?

The sales agreement will include the details about what is included and excluded in the property sale. There is the dwelling and the ground that it sits on. Sometimes there are parcels of land that change hands and right-of-ways (usage of land) that are granted to or received from adjoining land owners. Your deed must agree with the current status of the title. A closing company will verify these details; a survey may be ordered. The deed will be written to include details on the plot of land.

WHAT ARE THE OUTSTANDING DEBTS?

Once the preliminary work is complete, the closing agent will begin to order all the financial clearances that are required to successfully convey clear title. Any previous liens that have been placed on the property will either have to have been released or will be settled by withholding money from the seller at the closing. Tax certificates will have to be issued stating that all taxes are current, or they too will be withheld from the buyer. In areas with municipal water and sewage providers, those fees must also be paid. If the water and sewage are provided by a private company, they are not a closing issue. Then, finally, there is a mortgage payoff letter. If you are dealing with estate or distressed sellers, you may find that they take little or no money from the closing and may even owe more than they get. You may be able to resolve this by getting a creditor to make concessions, or the deal could fall through.

A seller who thinks that abandoning a property that is "under water" (a term used for one that owes more than it is worth) is an alternative should seek legal advice. Deficiencies in a mortgage may very well follow the individual once the property is sold.

THE BUYER NEEDS TO BRING MONEY

A number of items will have to be paid by the buyer at the closing, including the cost of the process, called closing fees. Items that are prorated, such as taxes, have been already paid by the seller. In addition, if there is a down payment or costs of the loan, such as points or bank fees, they will be due on the closing date and will have to be paid with a certified check.

The lawyer doing the closing (or the closing officer) will do all of the calculations of what is owed and to whom, and then they will issue a settlement sheet, referred to as a HUD-1. This standardized document will let the seller know what they will receive at the closing and the buyer know what is due from them. Regardless of what side of the deal you are on, you should review this document closely. If there are unexpected items, check them out before coming to the closing.

If you are the buyer, you will have to bring your funds in the form of a certified check because the closing agent will act as a disbursement agent as well. They will take the check of the buyer and issue checks to anyone else who is entitled to one. That may include the mortgage company, the taxing authorities and utilities, professionals, and then the balance to the seller. When this ritual is done, the deal is officially complete.

You will have many of these events in a successful real estate investment career, and no two will be exactly alike. Don't take any closings for granted, and hire good professionals to handle them for you.

CHAPTER 15

KEEPING THE SCORE

WADE'S STORY

Even though I had taken accounting in college, I really never learned how to keep business records. I was aware of their importance from the beginning, but because I was busy buying properties and wholesaling them, I thought that making the money was far more important than spending time with the details. Details have always been one of my biggest weaknesses. I tend to concentrate on the big picture and often overlook the small things. There are many good reasons to change that outlook, and I knew some of them from the day I started my business. Some, I have had to learn the hard way, which is not something I would recommend.

One of the reasons I was drawn into real estate was in part because of the tax benefits. I am able to use the depreciation deductions on my rented property to shelter most of my wholesale income. But the tax returns I have to file are inches thick, and compiling them takes extraordinarily detailed records. Having an accountant come in at the end of the year to make sense of it all can be very, very expensive. For me, I hadn't budgeted for that cost along the way. I have paid fees that have run into the tens of thousands of dollars, and I would not have had to do so if everything was in place on an ongoing basis. I am constantly working at putting new tools in place, mainly good software, and to improve the timeliness and accuracy of our in-house records.

I need information in order to make my decisions about how to manage and when to sell certain properties. The only way to do that in an informed way is to have accurate information on how specific properties are performing. I had a duplex that I thought was one of my best cash-flow producers, but for some reason, the utility, tax, and maintenance charges were being put on a property I owned one house away. When I discovered the error, I was not able to raise rents to cover the costs as I had Section 8 tenants in place on new leases, so I decided to sell. I had bought the place well, so I was able to make a profit on that transaction. I know that property analysis is something I need, and we are getting better at it.

Active investors are always looking for sources of financing. Banks require good financial records, and even private lenders need to know details about the condition of the buyer. I fill out personal financial statements on a regular basis, and I sign them certifying that the information is true. I need it to be accurate for a variety of reasons. Even if I am not interested in the nuts and bolts of the accounting aspect, I am very interested in the information it provides.

Record keeping is one of the more tedious elements of a real estate investment business, yet it remains one of the most critical. The number of transactions can be very substantial and how they are handled can become very complicated. If you start on the right track, you are more likely to stay on it. Your in-house system may be a simple one at the outset, even manual (handwritten) ledgers will work, but you need to be able to grow that system as the number of properties you own or the volume of deals you are doing increases.

START BY SEPARATING YOUR BUSINESS ACTIVITIES

One of the most important concepts for you to understand from the beginning is that different real estate activities result in different tax treatments, and you need to keep the activities separate in order to take advantage of available tax benefits. There is a difference between being an investor or a dealer in real estate. A dealer is the one who does the flipping or quick rehab of properties. The test is that you have purchased or taken control of a property with the idea of selling it, not holding it. The income you earn as a dealer will be taxed at the ordinary income tax rate and also incur the payment of the self-employment tax or FICA tax, which is currently 15.3 percent. Your profit working in these areas should be very high, but consider that you may pay as much as 40 percent–plus of it back in income and self-employment taxes.

For the property you purchase to hold as rentals, you are considered an investor and you will be able to defer much of your tax liability over the years and are likely to come up with a loss that will shelter your "dealer" income. All of the expense of operating this property is deductible as is the depreciation, which may exceed any profit. When you do sell this property, any increase in value (profit) will be taxed at the capital gains rate, not the ordinary income rate; deferring any or all of that tax is possible. Internal Revenue Code Section 1031 allows for a "like kind exchange." You need to consult with your accountant about your specific situation, but generally you may be able to use the money from the sale to purchase another property of equal or greater value and defer the gains you made from the sale of the first. You may even be able to do a partial exchange.

One of the tests is how long you held the first property—a period of two years seems to be the criteria—and you must act fairly quickly by identifying the property you intend to buy within 60 days of the sale and making the actual purchase within 180 days. Deferring taxes may give you the chance to build up a substantial net worth without any taxable implications until you liquidate your holdings. This opportunity is definitely worth serious consultation with a CPA.

CONSIDER MORE THAN ONE ENTITY

You may actually want to start more than one business as a way to segregate your activities, using one as the vehicle to act as a dealer of property and the other to act as a pure investor. Each of these entities will keep its own set of books and develop its own strategies. The business operating as a dealer will use primarily short-term lending instruments such as private money or lines of credit. The investing company will want long-term traditional financing such as mortgages. Both should be incorporated to protect you from a variety of liabilities. Whether you form an S Corporation or a limited liability company (LLC) is another area for your lawyer or accountant to advise you on. The time to make these decisions is when you are starting out.

TAKE ALL ALLOWABLE DEDUCTIONS

The tedious work of having a business is in the day-to-day record-keeping requirements. The benefit is that you can deduct the expenses of running that business from your taxable income. Know what the allowable deductions are, and keep accurate records. You should be able to deduct the cost of items purchased or used in order to operate your business, which can include a portion of the expense of your house if you use it for an office, the business use of your car and your computer, any educational seminars you attend, books or publications that you read, and all of your marketing expenses. You must keep accurate receipts and records, but the benefit is a greatly reduced tax burden.

KNOW WHAT YOU ARE EARNING

Each property must have a stand-alone profit and loss report. An astute investor needs to know if he or she is making or losing money on an ongoing basis. At times a loss happens as the result of a one-time expense for a repair or upgrade that will add to the value of the property and isn't likely to be repeated. Sometimes you may need to raise the rents to cover your increasing costs or to refinance your loan at a lower rate, to decrease the cost outflow. Certain properties start out at a breakeven but will appreciate greatly over time, giving you a substantial profit when you sell; even without positive cash flow, the rental income is paying down the mortgage. There are a vast number of scenarios to consider, but you won't know what to do unless you have adequate information.

KEEPING BOOKS AND RECORDS

Earlier, we mentioned that a manual journal might be adequate for a new investor, which is true. Using a single page to record transactions on a single property will provide a snapshot of how cash flow is going. But these days, many people keep their personal finances on a computer through Quickbooks or a simple checkbook program, so using the same system to manage your real estate accounting is a natural. The simpler general accounting programs such as Quickbooks and Peachtree can certainly be used effectively to handle what you need, but they will only really work if you sit down with a knowledgeable accountant and modify your chart of accounts to meet your needs. You must take care that you don't just enter data in a random fashion because, while you will accumulate accurate tax information, you will not receive good individual property management data.

If real estate investing becomes a full-time business for you, look into the specialized real estate software such as Tenant Pro, which will allow you to record your transactions on each property easily. Such software will also allow you to track the maintenance history of any property to prompt you to do preventative work in addition to the financial data. One of the most complicated areas is in setting up the property itself.

Much of the data from your original HUD-1 will have to be recorded. You need to track what you paid for the property itself as well as any of the closing expenses, because some of them are deductible. You need to record your mortgage payment and track what you pay in interest as well as principal, as only the interest is deductible. Real estate taxes that are also a tax deduction need to be paid on an ongoing basis. Setting up a property the right way is easier than changing it later and trying to recapture all of the information that has been missed.

The cost of this work will be a good bit cheaper if you manage it on a day-to-day basis and have your accountant verify it on a quarterly basis. You will then have good profit and loss statements to check and be ready to go to your bank with updated information whenever you need it.

Record keeping is never the fun side of the business, but it is the place where you keep score. The only way to win is to understand the numbers.

CHAPTER 16

KNOW WHEN TO HOLD THEM AND KNOW WHEN TO FOLD THEM

WADE'S STORY

I am constantly thinking about all of my deals and all of the properties that I own. Some of them that seem great going in start to develop problems that take away some of the attraction. I go over it time and time again in my head, wondering whether to go forward or whether to cut my losses and walk. I have developed fairly good instincts, some of them learned the hard way—directly out of my pocket.

Wholesale deals can slide around on thin ice occasionally, because distressed sellers don't always tell you everything. The search before closing often uncovers liens and tax debt that weren't completely disclosed. I will try to work through it because as long as there is any room at the end, I will make some profit. Some never close, and I can usually think back to the moment I realized that might happen. It usually doesn't pay for me to walk away earlier.

I will do some deals for my own account that are from distressed sellers, and here I am not just an observer in the transaction. I am the buyer. I've made an offer for the property because I think I can rent it for a positive cash flow, and I see the potential appreciation. But if the debt goes higher because the purchase price goes up, my cost will go up, and then I have a decision to make. The most difficult is when the seller finds out that there will be no cash for them at the closing, and they are very disappointed to say the least. I am sympathetic but sometimes I can do little other than take money out of my own pocket. Sometimes I will, and sometimes I walk away so I don't have to say no.

When a property I own starts to cause trouble, the pressure goes up. The problems may result from previously undiscovered mechanical trouble, serious tenant disputes, or chronic vacancies. I have had tenants in a duplex who had ongoing arguments and who tried to put me in the middle and a tenant who fought off eviction for months and months. Such situations make me wonder if the property is worth it.

But the worst was a purchase of five properties from another private investor I had been looking to do business with for some time. All of them were in the need of dire rehab, and none were close to my typical areas. Cash was tight and there was no room for the unforeseen. I thought if I took these five over, it would mean some future deals. All had been previously foreclosed on, and I was offered 100 percent financing with some extra cash available to do the fix-ups, but it wasn't nearly enough. I was overaggressive and overconfident, I believe now. I never did get them habitable, and I had to pay out on the loans as well as all of the other overhead. Positive cash flow from my other properties was being drained off.

At first I hated to admit I was wrong. I tried everything I could think of, but it didn't work. After long deliberation and advice from my business consultant, Suzanne, we met with the private lender and discussed a deal for him to take the properties back. He reluctantly agreed because he didn't want to foreclose on them, and he even told me that he respected the fact that I came to him instead of avoiding the situation. No book or seminar I had been around taught me how to handle this problem.

This was a humbling experience and an expensive one as well. I had paid out almost $100,000 and had absolutely nothing to show for it. But ending this cash drain on my business was a great help, and the learning was valuable.

Even consistently profitable businesses come up with lemons from time to time. Does anyone remember new Coke, which was launched and then removed before it damaged the entire soft drink dynasty? This happens with investments in the market and with real estate as well. Some investors miss the signs, and some people are so caught up in the excitement of acquisition that they ignore some potentially damaging situations.

There are deals you shouldn't make. Owning any real estate is not better than owning a bad piece of property. When you are a new investor trying to leverage little or none of your own cash, you can be too eager because you think it "isn't costing me anything." All cashless deals are not winners, and those that are being sold by other investors rather than a motivated seller should be scrutinized. In an active real estate market, why would another investor turn over a deal without any cash? Most experienced businesspeople know that the only money that is sure is what you receive up front. Look for undisclosed problems.

If the property is unrented or in need of serious repair, consider that once it is in your name, it will be costing you real money. In addition to those "easy" payments, you will have taxes and utilities and perhaps repairs, without offsetting income. You need to analyze deals carefully from the time you make your first one, because some are better left undone.

PROTECTING YOURSELF PERSONALLY

By this point, you should have formed a business entity to own and manage your property so that your personal assets will be safe from most liability. Lawsuits are a fact of business. A corporate entity means that the only assets at risk are those owned by the company. After you have accumulated a large real estate portfolio, that amount may still be substantial, but your risk will end without touching your personal holdings, including your residence.

If you are interested in the purchase of a larger property such as an apartment building, which may have a higher risk but a greater opportunity, you may want to consider an entirely separate entity for that purchase alone. You can seal off all of the risk and the liability with that corporate shell. If something goes amiss, you may even be able to just walk away without an exposure to other holdings.

COMMUNICATE ABOUT PROBLEMS

Sometimes you have certain properties that are costing too much, bringing in too little, and taking too much of your time. You may simply be able to sell out and perhaps even break even. If there is too much debt owing on the property, you may need to put out actual cash at closing, but at least the cash drain will stop. If the problem is that you paid too much to the seller and they are still holding the financing, you may be able to deed it back and cancel out the indebtedness. If you don't make payments and the loan goes into default, your creditor has the right to begin foreclosure and regain control of the property, which is both a costly and a time-consuming process. You may volunteer to simply return ownership to cancel out the debt and relieve you from further financial obligations. You may need to add some additional payments as an incentive.

Casino gambling is a very profitable business for the casino. Much of their profit is contributed by gamblers who are losing and keep playing to try to break even. That's not a prudent way to play blackjack or to be a real estate investor. If the lawyers, accountants, closing agents, contractors, appraisers, and bird-dogs all around you are getting rich, but you're floundering, you know it's time for a change.

17

BUILDING AN EMPIRE

WADE'S STORY

When I began as an investor, my expectations were high, even though I wasn't sure exactly where high could go. I knew I could earn a nice living and build for my own future, but the more I became involved, the more opportunities opened up, and I was always interested in what others had to say. First I was approached by a mortgage banker who asked me if I wanted to originate loans for him. This goes beyond a referral; it involves handling some of the paperwork as well, particularly the completed first application. He would place the loan and pay me 50 percent of the fee. I was out in the marketplace anyway, and this made great sense.

I was interested for reasons beyond the income. I wanted a chance to learn that business as well, because getting a mortgage was critical to my deals. But the money wasn't bad. One month before I even left the gas company, I earned $8,000 as my portion of his fees. There are laws governing this activity, so check out the ones in your state before you start. These days, I am in the brokering business with a few partners, and now I am out looking for investors to refer business to me.

My other major side business also began casually. I was borrowing a lot of hard money to finance new projects, and when the work was complete, I often did my permanent financing with the same savings and loan. That's how I met Spencer Hirshberg, the lawyer who handled the closings for the bank. A lawyer with twenty-five years of experience, Spencer became very curious about how I was borrowing the initial money to buy properties so quickly. He started asking me questions, and every time I showed up, he was more interested. Then he began to see one of my friends show up regularly as well, and he was anxious to get involved. We had been paying ten points and 15 percent on this short-term money, and Spencer offered to make us loans for eight points and the same interest. He was being cautious because this was new to him. We were so excited about having our "own" private investor, we didn't negotiate. The bonus was saving two points.

After a few deals, Spencer's comfort level was going up. My friend John and I told him that we knew other investors who were looking to purchase property with private money. This had been profitable for Spencer, and now that we could form a business, his face lit up more than the sun. He loves deals as much as I do. So Spencer and my friend John Walker and I formed a partnership and created Community Investment Group Ltd. We have expanded our pool of money past Spencer's investment to include lines of credit with the bank, and we can borrow at market rates and lend out at much higher returns. The investor gets the advantage of quick access to capital to get a project going, and we never lend more than 65 percent of a project, so our investment is always protected. The private money we use gets an excellent return secured by a mortgage. Our foreclosure rate is low, and our profits have been consistently high.

My next venture was another natural. Once I had gone through the overly costly reinstall of six furnaces at one time (described earlier), I began to pay attention to the cost of heating and cooling. In 1998, I spent over $50,000 on my own properties alone and knew other investors who were spending as much. Within eighteen months, I had formed my own heating and cooling business in an effort both to save money and give me immediate access to a technician for my own emergencies. The business is there, but managing it. . . .

My most recent off-shoot venture has been a seminar business that also has a mentoring program and some educational tapes. Success Productions began in 2003, and this book is a result of that venture. As an active wholesaler, I meet many investors who have all kinds of questions. My partner Suzanne and I created the first seminar to answer some of them, but that actually created more interest. So now we mentor small groups and help them get through their first couple of deals. Many of them buy property from me as well.

You will likely run into a number of folks who would like to partner with you, and you may even be able to find someone as knowledgeable and interested as Spencer Hirshberg. I have been very lucky along the way. Keep your eyes open for these opportunities, but remember that real estate is your main career.

Real estate investment is a vibrant business. People involved in it spend a substantial amount of money on other goods and services. An aggressive player can find some or a lot of extra income by referring, promoting, or actually becoming involved in a number of these areas. But remember that your main focus must be your real estate deals, so don't let other interests drain your resources—either financial or human.

MORTGAGE BROKERING

On the face of it, mortgage brokering is a fairly straightforward business. You match borrowers with lenders, whether they are traditional bankers or private money sources. You are paid a commission on the total loan you refer, which can range from 0.5 percent to 3 percent. This fee is paid at the time the loan closes. This work can be occasionally time consuming because you will be responsible for the paperwork, which means that you take the initial application and then find a lender who is willing to make the loan. Most brokers work for a variety of companies who lend, although some only work for one. Then back-up paperwork will be required, and you may have to work closely with the borrower to make sure they submit it as required. A few missing pieces of documentation, and the loan won't close and you won't get paid.

In many states, you have to be licensed to be a mortgage broker. Check out the requirements first. If you are selling the property as well, you need to be careful about being open with your client so he or she understands that you are being compensated by the mortgage company. They might want to do the money deal elsewhere. You can also participate by referring customers to a broker and drawing a fee from the broker. Again, be up front with your clients. Their real estate business is what is valuable to you, and your reputation is critical.

PRIVATE MONEY LENDING

As a loan broker, you are likely to have an affiliation with private money sources, but the best way to be involved in this area is to be one of the actual lenders. If you have some ready cash available, you could leverage it with some bank money or you could find a well-heeled private investor who would like to partner with you. The returns here are substantial. You may borrow at 5 percent and lend at 12 percent, and you collect loan points as well. The loans are secured by a mortgage on the property, but you will quickly learn that it is never cheap to get the collateral back instead of the payments. So, make the loans carefully. You may have looser credit standards than traditional lenders, but you need to explore the reliability of your borrower and monitor their loan and progress closely.

What you will bring to this venture is a supply of customers and a knowledge of the local real estate market. Private lenders often make deals on ugly houses—those that need work—but you must make a knowledgeable inspection first to find out if the project seems reasonable. If it doesn't look doable, your borrower may abandon it along the way.

Some really sophisticated investors may try to pool private investment money from a variety of individuals and use this to start a private lending group. There is a good chance that this activity falls under banking or security laws in most states and will thus require a substantial amount of professional advice. Do you really want to manage this kind of ambitious venture? Profits may be good, but the work level and liability are high.

PROPERTY MANAGEMENT

You will be managing your own property when you start out, so you will have a firsthand look at what this type of business involves. The first element is in keeping the units rented and then collecting and recording all of the rent payments, but the most difficult aspect is in taking care of maintenance and repair. You will field all the tenant calls and determine what is an emergency and what is a general complaint. Water leaking could lead to a disaster and no heat is serious, but a nonworking light may just be an annoyance. You need to be able to respond to these calls and dispatch the proper maintenance personnel or contractor to handle the work. Staff requirements may be high for fees that run as low as 5 percent of the total rent revenue to a high of perhaps 10 percent. Your fees will depend on the level of service you can provide, and all contractor extras will be billed to the property owner in addition. You will likely add your fee to these charges.

This type of business will not be profitable without a fairly large number of units to manage—at least over one hundred and perhaps upwards of two hundred to get to a breakeven if the rents in your area are on the lower side. Work the numbers before you decide. If the average rent of the units you could manage is $800 and you can charge a fee of 8 percent, your property management revenue will be $84 per month per unit. Determine how many units you need to set up an office and hire enough personnel to staff it adequately. Consider the rent, salaries, benefits, and the rest of the overhead before you even draw any profits.

Finally, ask yourself, what are your real strengths and can you manage this type of business easily? Is this the best use of your time? The one reason it may be worthwhile is if you have acquired a substantial number of rental properties for yourself and have other reasons, such as some mortgage business, to develop your own administrative staff. While they are doing your own work, doing it for other investors as well may be profitable. Be cautious, though, about becoming involved in labor-intensive businesses.

START A MAINTENANCE OR CONTRACTING BUSINESS

Perhaps one day you will total up what you are spending on maintenance, heating, or even rehab construction and decide that you might as well start a business to cover your own work as well as that of others. Before you get into this, remember that you need to have at least some expertise about any type of business before you go into it, so if you are not an accomplished handyman, this idea may not be a good one. You need to be able to profitably estimate the cost of the work, schedule and supervise the people who are doing it, and make sure the jobs are completed as you planned. This work takes time and expertise. It may be easier for a contractor to develop a real estate portfolio than for an investor to start a contracting company.

What you may want to consider is a partnership with a craftsman or technician who wants to be in an independent business. You can share the financial investment and provide a steady stream of customers, and your partner can manage the actual work. In the end that arrangement should prove profitable, and you can both share in those profits.

TEACHING AND MENTORING

Once you have your investment business up and running, you will find that you are educating new investors all of the time. This area of opportunity interests a lot of people. Some will call just to "kick the tires" and never make a purchase, while others will become regular customers. At some point, you may feel that you want to charge for your expertise. Again, in this case you need to match your expertise with the opportunity.

The seminar business can be very profitable for a high-profile speaker. Having fifty people in a room pay $500 for a one-day seminar gives you revenue of $25,000, with expenses that are likely to be less than $3,000. The weekend boot camps charge $4,000 to $5,000 per person and can have thirty-plus attendees, which means your income exceeds $100,000! This business is obviously very lucrative.

The costs here are primarily in advertising and marketing, and you will have to front them in the beginning until you build a reputation. Having platform skills are critical, and you can hire an event planner to handle the rest of the details.

Tapes and books go along with the seminar business. The gross revenue is less than the actual seminars, but once they have been completed, the income is more passive and may not require the travel that a seminar business does. Use the Internet and direct mail as methods of marketing.

Charging for mentoring or consulting is yet another stream of revenue. Most new investors could benefit from having someone walk them through their first purchase, giving advice and encouragement. You also have incentives to do this for free because if you are a wholesaler, this activity offers a steady supply of customers for the properties you locate. However, you may want to limit the people who have access to you on a regular basis; charging a reasonable fee and setting guidelines is a good way to accomplish this.

Interest in real estate investment is at an all-time high and shows little sign of slowing down. A serious new investor can profit handsomely from this activity, but it takes time and effort. Your focus early on in your venture should remain on real estate investing. Many side ventures will be offered, or you may decide to develop them on your own. Just remember to take care of your property before you do anything else.

CHAPTER 18

FOLLOW YOUR GUT

WADE'S STORY

The first investment seminar I attended was in Orlando, Florida, and I paid $5,000 to go to it. At the time, I didn't have the extra money to spend, so I put it on my credit card. Why not, the seminar material promised a quick return? In addition to the enrollment fee, I had plane fare and five nights in a hotel to cover. Unfortunately, the quick return never happened, and I ended up paying for it over many months.

I was first drawn in by a free seminar that was offered at a local hotel. The speaker was so good and made everything sound so easy, I thought I couldn't afford not to go. Of the seventy-five people in the room, twenty-five signed up. The topic was note brokering. I didn't know anything about it, but it sounded like a winner and faster cash than I was making just investing in rental properties.

I was amazed to see almost one thousand people in the room in Orlando, all as eager as me, and many of them looked as if they had used some of their last dollars to be there, which was about what I had done. The same promotional seminars had been given all over the country, and we were all warned that there was only "limited seating" available in Orlando. Our shared dream was financial independence, but I think the only ones who achieved it were our hosts.

With no individual attention and only a few of our questions answered, I looked around at a sea of faces, young and old, and most of them looked a bit confused. I have wondered how many of the people in that room achieved anything close to that financial independence or even made any money at all. I'll bet a lot came home like me, fired up at first, but after a couple of days, most of us getting caught up in our daily lives and forgetting about living our dreams.

Did I waste my money? I felt so at the time, and I am sure I wasn't alone. But over time, I realized that what I really took away was an even larger vision than I had before I came. I still remember all the days at my job at the gas company, going in and out of people's homes just knowing that this work would only be temporary. As I was walking, I was thinking about the ways I could better myself. I knew it started with more education, and by now I have realized that education without application won't do a thing for you. The new investor has to make that first deal. Experience is the best teacher, along with some guidance from someone who has done it. It's not just having dreams, it's living them.

I often think about the difference between the people who make it in all fields, not just real estate, and those who do not. From my vantage point, the difference is not that big. I am going to devote the rest of this chapter to some of the lessons I have learned, starting with my sports career, that carried over to my life in real estate. I was practically raised on sports, and valuable lessons in that world can easily be used in the business world.

The number-one thing I've seen in successful people is confidence. If you don't believe in yourself, how can you expect someone else to? I learned the power of confidence from one of my college teammates. He probably doesn't even realize how much of an influence he had on my life. A year ahead of me, we played the same position on the varsity basketball team. He wasn't big, wasn't fast, and couldn't really jump, but he believed that he was the best player in the world. He would always be talking in practice about how he was going to jump over somebody in the game and dunk the ball. Not likely, he couldn't dunk in practice. We just listened to him talk. But when the lights came on and it was game time, there he was going over someone and making a dunk. He was almost always there when we needed him.

Years later, I figured it out. He was telling us what he was going to do so he could believe it himself. You'll find that when you say out loud that you are going to do something, you are more inclined to get it done. The more you learn to believe in yourself, the more your mind and body will figure out a way to get it done. I have now seen many people accomplish things other people doubted they could do, simply because they believed in themselves.

For real estate investors, confidence is a must. It takes a confident person to ask a seller to take 50 percent of the value of the house, even when you know they are unlikely to get much more. If you feel a bit challenged in this area, you can start off with something small but make sure it is a bit more than you have done before. Build on small successes, whether it's making a cold call on your first seller, making the first real offer, or approaching a private lender for money. Each success will build confidence, and the next time it will be easier. Back yourself up with education so you know at least as much and likely more than the person you are dealing with. The time is fast approaching for you to take some risk.

Successful people are not afraid to fail. They see it as part of the game: win some, lose some, but you will win none if you never play. In my mind, not trying is the biggest failure of all.

I was a fairly big high school basketball star in my area, and fans from other teams often showed up just to cheer against me. I seldom paid any attention until the night we lost a game because I missed a foul shot. I was considered one of the county's best players—a guy who made 85 percent of my foul shots—and in that critical game I went zero for seven, and we lost the game as a result. Fans from the other side were beaming with pleasure, and I can still remember it. The ride home was endless. I felt I had let my team as well as the whole school down, and I didn't want to show my face there the next day. But the sun came up again and I went back to school and to practice, and after, I spent extra time working on my foul shot. It was coming back and the very next game I made ten out of eleven, scored forty-six points, and my team was on its way to the playoffs.

My point is that it is okay to fail. No one succeeds every time. When you do, you need to learn from your mistakes and come back even stronger. I could have let the bad game ruin my season, but I worked through it and actually came out a better foul shooter, and now, I realize, a better person.

Every deal is not a winner, and some may cause you painful losses. You'll make mistakes, but even more important is how you recover. I've seen many investors give up after a few deals when they didn't go perfectly. If I had quit, I would still be at the gas company, maybe. Almost everyone who was there with me only eight years ago is gone. These days, corporate jobs offer far less security than they did in the past; there is risk everywhere. Even corporate jobs have become a low-security risk as well.

Every successful person is motivated by something; they may turn the smallest event into a motivational tool that drives them to succeed. You need to figure out what motivates you, whether it's freedom, money, or personal satisfaction. You may be driven to overcome a difficult childhood, a competitive sibling, or an ex-spouse who thinks you can't succeed alone. Learn to turn a negative into a positive.

I still think back to my days at the gas company when one of my friends and I first started buying property. Other guys at work were laughing at us, calling us slumlords to our face and probably worse behind our backs. They derided us, saying we were just asking for trouble. I saw that the real trouble was expecting someone to give you a salary for the next thirty years, and I was right. Many of them are gone, and the others are stuck at what I realize is a dead end.

Remembering those guys laughing at me has served as one of my motivations. Every time I am down or things aren't going well, I remember how boring that job was and how many goals I still have for myself.

There are always going to be doubters. I love it when somebody tells me I can't do something. This gives me added incentive to succeed. I make a mental note and then find new ways to figure it out. That becomes my personal challenge, and it should be yours. I always hear from folks who haven't done it, that you can't buy property at 60 percent of its value, but I continue to find ways to do so. Then I envision the look on the faces of the ones who said it doesn't happen. Maybe I'm lucky that everyone doesn't believe it.

I think creating a plan for financial security is important. The days of working a job until you retire, which is what my parents did, are over.

Some friends of mine are perfect examples. They both had good airline jobs and lived comfortably with plans to retire early and enjoy their grandchildren while taking advantage of their travel benefits. Now in their fifties, their plans have changed radically. The airline downturn seriously affected their company stock and their 401(k), and they've taken a 30 percent pay cut. Now, instead of slowing down, they are working second jobs. Their bright future has turned to uncertainty.

If this couple had bought some properties over the years and held them, they would have likely been paid for by now. Cash flow would have been steady, and their nest egg would have not only been intact, it would have grown.

The bottom line is that real estate provides options and opportunities, for the present as well as the future.

My main message is to remember that whatever you do, whether investing in real estate or not, you should follow your best instincts. If a deal doesn't feel right, it probably isn't. If you meet someone who puts you on alert, they may not be the right client or advisor. If a house doesn't feel right, don't buy it. Sometimes things happen so fast, you don't have time to think; you just have to react. This is the time to rely on your gut feelings.

I am living proof that anything is possible, as long as you are willing to work for it. Success doesn't discriminate; it is available to everyone who believes in themselves. And the help is there as well. Mike Wheeler happened to answer my call. Spencer Hirshberg was a great connection who was there at the right time. Suzanne and I met when I needed someone like her and wanted to expand my work with a book and seminars. I believe that if you put yourself in a position to succeed, God will give you the tools and bring you the people necessary to make it happen.

Good luck and happy investing!
Wade Timmerson
November 2003

EPILOGUE

SUZANNE'S TURN

When I first began this journey almost two years ago, I was only an observer. A CPA I had only recently met referred me to Wade Timmerson as a possible business advisor. My experience came from my life as a business owner for twenty years. I have written numerous books for entrepreneurs and have been a consultant for companies in many different types of businesses. Some businesses, such as manufacturing and retail, are very straightforward. Some are a bit trickier, such as restaurants and hi-tech start-ups. I even worked with a real estate development company in Little Rock, Arkansas, which was tough from beginning to end. Wade was the first real estate investor I had met, and I came in a bit skeptical. Having seen the late night TV ads and all of the hype, I was sure that the promises of wealth were overblown.

I know there isn't such a thing as easy money, and the only truly passive income is an inheritance or lottery winnings. There are few real businesses anyone can get into with little or no money and become successful on the basis of hard work and tenacity. Interestingly, after a few months with Wade, I began to change my mind. He had done it; starting out with almost no cash, he began acquiring properties as rentals, doing some rehabs and primarily flipping deals to other investors, and he had amassed an amazing portfolio of properties and a history of strong performance, with his share of mistakes as well. That was why I was there: to see if I could uncover some of the more difficult problems and find solutions. So, even if I saw the possibilities, I wondered if anyone could do this without creating some traps for themselves along the way. But Wade understood his own missteps and why they had happened, even if he wasn't sure how to undo them.

One of his earliest mistakes was to have borrowed short-term money for long-term projects. A few times, also, he had taken more equity out of a property than he should have. That was resolved by some serious conversation with his bankers and selling a few properties to help. Another mistake early on was a series of nonperforming properties bought from another investor, which had been overpriced and overfinanced. We returned title as the first part of our deal with him and have been working on a settlement. Neither of these problems were life threatening, but they were—and are—easy traps for a new investor to fall into. As I began to work more closely with Wade, I had a growing respect for him as a business owner who was as open and honest with me as he was in sharing with other new investors how to start out right and keep from creating situations that would cost them money and grief. Like the Pied Piper, Wade was developing quite a following. He knew that I wrote books on business and did a good number of seminars, and he started talking to me about wanting to do the same. I like what I do now, and the fact that I have always used a "been there, done that" perspective. I just wasn't sure the public wanted to hear the real story. Many of the existing books and seminars promised great wealth with no money down, and they talk too little about the work involved. Would anyone pay to hear the *real* story?

As 2003 began, Wade and I had already been trying to develop a book, and I was busy at work on it. We both decided that a seminar would be the next thing to try. Encouraging us was someone who had been working on a $5,000-per-person program, and again the enrollees heard the promise of great riches. I don't subscribe to it, and neither did Wade, so we went another route.

We designed an all-day seminar featuring Wade's A Team of advisors: legal, accounting, agent, appraiser, and so on. Wade and I both spoke about our views of the real estate business. Again, his candidness won the day, and our audience was thrilled. Many had paid ten times elsewhere what we charged for our programs, but they kept telling us that they learned more during the day with us than anywhere else. This topic was clearly a natural for a book, but I still had a question about how anyone could turn out to be a successful investor. *Was it all an illusion*, I wondered?

Wade makes it look easy. He is open and friendly and always networking. People want to do business with him. He is very confident and tries new ideas easily to see if they work. He is also very competitive—a natural streak enhanced by his years playing basketball. Wade could succeed in any business, because he loves the game and welcomes the risk.

At our first seminar, I saw a few eager faces paying absolutely rapt attention to every word. At the end of the long day, some of them seemed more familiar, but not ones I remembered until I began seeing one of our students at Wade's office virtually every time I was there. His name was Dave, and he became a mentoring student of Success Productions, our education business. He became a star pupil, so I did learn a good bit about him.

Dave Mackowick has a day job (actually a night job) for a local utility company. He had already tried a previous side business before and done well at it, but it was seasonal. With a wife and two kids, he needed to be concerned about financial stability. In early 2003, he began his real estate venture borrowing money on the equity on his house and buying a single family house as rental property. It was a bargain, sold on a wholesale deal by Wade, and that's how Dave found out about our seminar. He is an enthusiastic learner, and his wife is very supportive of his work at building financial security for the family. Since that first purchase, Dave has become very aggressive, buying a few four-unit properties as well as one three-unit, a duplex, and a number of single-family homes. In eight months, he has acquired twenty-three units and as I write this, twenty-one are rented. Some were ready when he bought them, and some had to be fixed before they could be rented. Dave knows how to get the job done.

None of the invested cash came directly from Dave's pocket. All of the purchases were financed by his home equity line of credit, then a small business line of credit. For the short-term fix-ups, he used Wade's private money group. Then when the work was done, he converted to conventional S&L financing. He has only recently slowed down on his acquisitions, but this is how he changed his circumstance: His net worth has climbed by well over $100,000, and his positive cash flow is in excess of $2,500 per month. Three of the houses are under agreement to sell as a rent-to-own and his profits will exceed $40,000 although they may take up to a year to close. Not bad in less than a year!

More importantly, Dave loves it and plans to make the transition to full-time involvement. Dave has learned to do it all. He buys to fix up, to rent, and to flip. He is also becoming a part of our seminar company, not yet a great public speaker but a generous and supportive mentor to others. Most importantly, he is living proof to me of the possibilities, as well as of the confidence you see growing along with success.

So I was becoming a believer, with first Wade and then Dave. Time to try a little of this myself. I didn't actually plan to do it, but it was a good learning experience and I just might do a bit more. The investment property I bought was being sold by an estate that was under the control of the daughter of the deceased. It was a small, modest house in a small community, and the daughter couldn't wait to get the estate settled. The house needed a little bit of work, and she had no intentions of putting any money into it. The debts of the estate were already higher than our offer for the property, but it was the only offer she had. A lawyer handled the probate, took a lot of time, charged a fairly high fee, and had not acted quickly enough to avoid one of the creditors putting a lien on the estate. This was a textbook distressed sale. At the same time, I knew that I was also solving a problem for the seller. She was able to negotiate with creditors so that they took their portion of the funds that came out of the house and settled all claims, and she even earned a fee as executrix. She wasn't entirely happy, but she was clearly relieved.

I was also able to experience the circus of a closing. Many of them turn out to look like that to the casual observer—days of nothing happening and then everyone running around like crazy, getting paperwork ready in the minutes before the event is to take place. Mine was on, then off, and then on again. The sellers had a long drive and they weren't happy, but a few missing documents had the closing agent turning around to go somewhere else because ours was not ready and then turning around again. I know a good bit about business transactions, but this ritual was more than slightly confusing to me. Paperwork requirements were extensive, and I signed my name on everything. Usually checks are disbursed to the seller if there is money coming, but the closing agent did not have them with him this day. A reputable agent can be trusted to send them, but in this case, my seller drove another hour away to pick them up. The sellers were worn out from the process, but they did shake my hand at the end.

And at the end, I was the owner of a house for which I had paid about half of the appraisal value, which I did a few weeks later. I paid cash and didn't need an appraisal. My tenants were moved in immediately, and the yearly rent was a return of over 25 percent of the price less my expense of property tax and insurance, which was about 6 percent. I had a 19 percent return and a tenant who hoped to buy the place within the year for close to the appraisal value. Their monthly cost would then go down, and they would own the place. Wow, this really does work.

Well, most of the time it does. What it takes is some work looking for the right situations and making a careful deal. Check out the area and the condition of your purchase. Develop good professional relationships and use them. You need a good lawyer and accountant to help you close your deals and record your expenses properly. Find a good professional real estate agent, and work with that agent to find property. You need a service-driven insurance agent, and make sure the insurer covers you as soon as you own a property and that the coverage is complete. Develop good contracting resources, and pay attention to the work that is being done on your behalf. Pay your bills promptly, or at least try to, and if you can't pay it all, pay part and be available.

Real estate is not the easy-money or get-rich-quick scheme that some ads and seminars promote, but it can provide an absolutely great opportunity to build assets in many ways. You can make money when you make the deal, because your goal is to buy a property at less than its market value. Do not take that money out at the closing in the form of a loan. You can make money on positive cash flow from rentals that exceed your out-of-pocket expense, and you can make money by paying down debt at the same time the value of your property grows. At the end of the day, a solid investor can build a substantial nest egg for retirement. Becoming a millionaire is possible here for people who would never do it any other way.

But there are risks and inevitable setbacks. They are a fact of life. Earlier, we discussed that you could find some bargains from disillusioned investors, which doesn't mean they have run into a complete disaster. It may be a major repair that is taking more money than they have or a series of frustrating tenant disasters. This is a long-term game, and while some short-term players may win, most will tie at best.

Wade is particularly tenacious, and he has a great faith in what he is trying to accomplish. Dave Mackowick shows signs of the same traits. I know they both will succeed. I also now know that the possibilities are endless. This business has a never-ending supply of buyers and sellers, and when one deal is missed, another one presents itself.

My best advice is that even if you feel confident after reading this book, read a few more. Take some seminars, talk to others who are doing it, and find or hire a mentor if you can. There is a learning curve here, and you will need guidance. Wade and I both would be happy to hear from you. We can give you some encouragement along the way and perhaps help you to find answers to your questions.

This book has centered around Wade's story—all of it true and all of it meant to help the reader understand all of the aspects of real estate investment, particularly when it involves fields (such as law and accounting) that are likely to be unfamiliar. You must learn some of the basics of both. You may only be investing on the side, but this will never be just a hobby. It is a business.

If Success Productions is holding a seminar in your town, we hope you will stop by and meet us. Or feel free to contact us at Suzanne@SuzanneCaplan.com or Wade@WadeTimmerson.com. I sincerely echo Wade's words: Good luck and happy investing.

Suzanne Caplan
November 2003

GLOSSARY

Adjustable-Rate Mortgage (ARM): A mortgage with an interest rate and payment that change periodically depending on the terms of the loan.

Agreement of Sale: A contract that obligates the buyer to purchase a property and a seller to sell the property. Includes all terms and conditions of that sale.

Amortization: A term used to describe the allocation of a loan over a predetermined period of time at a specific interest rate. The amortization of a loan includes payment of interest and a portion of the outstanding principal balance during each payment cycle.

Appraisal: A professional estimate of value of a property, usually done by a licensed appraiser. It is based on similar recent sales in the area and takes into consideration condition and upgrades on the property.

Appreciation: The increase in value of a property over time.

ARV (After Repair Value): The estimated value of a property after the repairs have been completed; what it would be worth in the market in excellent condition.

Assignment: An agreement that gives the buyer of a property the ability to transfer their rights of an agreement to someone else.

Assumption of Mortgage: A clause in the mortgage agreement that gives a buyer the right to take over an existing mortgage.

Balloon Payment: A loan with monthly payments based on a thirty-year amortization schedule where the unpaid principal balance is due in a lump sum payment at the end of a specific period (usually five or seven years). Many of these mortgages contain an option to reset the interest rate to the current market rate and to extend the maturity date provided certain conditions are satisfied.

Beneficiary: The recipient of money or benefits from a will or an agreement.

Bird Dog: A person who goes out to scout available properties for an investor and is compensated in return when a deal is made for the purchase.

Capital Gain: The tax description of the profit that is made on a property at the time of sale, often deducting the cost of improvements and purchase price.

Cash Flow: The difference between the cash at the beginning of a period and the cash at the end. This amount may be increased by the sale of assets or decreased by the purchase of assets.

Chain of Title: The ownership history of a property, particularly anything affecting title. Any irregularities along the way may cause a title to be in dispute.

Collateral: A tangible asset that is pledged and encumbered for the payment of a loan. The asset may remain in the possession of the borrower but under the control of the lender.

Commission: The fee paid to an individual for one's services, usually a percentage of the value of a transaction.

Comparable: A property used to determine the value of another property; usually under similar conditions and in the same general area.

Conditional Sales Contract: A sales contract that will not be enforceable unless certain conditions are met.

Confession of Judgment: A phrase that describes a clause in a loan agreement permitting the lender to record a lien of the assets of the borrower without having to bring suit in court. This clause will normally trigger when there is a default.

Contract: An agreement between two parties that is legally enforceable. May be written or oral as long as there is an understanding between the parties and an exchange of consideration.

Cosigner: Any signator to a note, other than the primary signator, who is fully obligated to the terms of the note until it is paid.

Debt Service: Includes both the principal and the interest of any loan; the total payment due.

Deed: The legal documents that define the ownership of a property, conveying title and recording any exceptions and encumbrances.

Default: The failure to make timely payment of a debt, which results in a loan being called in by the bank.

Deficiency: Any shortfall between the proceeds of a forced sale and the amount owed on a note.

Depreciation: The decrease in value of a property over time and scheduled for tax purposes.

Due on Sale: A clause in a mortgage that triggers the balance of the loan to be paid immediately upon sale of the property.

Earnest Money: Also "hand money." A down payment that shows good faith that a buyer intends to purchase a property; applied to the purchase price of the property. It is normally nonrefundable if the sale is not completed, unless there is a contingency clause.

Equity: The difference between the value of an asset and the total liabilities. For the purpose of determining the current worth of property, the current sale value should be used.

Escrow: The holding of money or documents by a neutral third party prior to closing. It can also be an account held by the lender (or servicer) into which a homeowner pays money for taxes and insurance.

Estate: The complete or partial ownership in real property.

Eviction: The process of a landlord legally removing a tenant for not meeting contractual obligations.

Executor: The person in charge of making decisions and paying taxes, expenses, and bequests pertaining to an estate.

FHA (Federal Housing Administration): A government agency that insures mortgages to protect approved lenders from losses that may occur if a borrower defaults on a loan.

5/1 ARM: An adjustable-rate mortgage where the interest rate is fixed for five years and then adjusted every five years thereafter.

Fixed Rate: Describes a loan that is written for a single interest rate for the entire term.

Flipping: Also known as "wholesaling," buying and selling properties to other investors for a quick profit. Contracts are usually assigned to the buyer who will close on them.

Foreclosure: The legal proceedings when a bank lender or other creditor takes back a property because of default in payment or terms.

Grace Period: The period of time between the payment due date and the date when the payment is considered late.

Hard Money: Also known as "private money"; money loaned by a private individual (not a bank) at rates higher than conventional loans with minimal qualifications.

HUD-1 Settlement Statement (HUD): A final listing of the costs of a mortgage transaction. It provides the sales price, the down payment, as well as the total settlement costs required from the buyer and seller.

Installment Sale: A transaction when the property transfers from one owner to another for the payment over time of the agreed price.

Joint Tenancy: The shared interest in property of two or more persons with the right of survivorship.

Judgment: An encumbrance as the result of the decision of a court which, once recorded, becomes a lien on real property.

Land Contract: An instrument that allows control of a property to remain with the buyer while leaving ownership with the seller until all agreed-to payments have been made.

Land Trust: A trust used primarily to hold title to real estate without disclosure of the actual owner. The trustee is the title holder, but the undisclosed beneficiaries have the control and may also revoke the trust.

Lessee: The person renting the property from a landlord.

Lessor: The person renting the property to a tenant; the landlord.

Lien: Any encumbrance against the title to property, such as a mortgage or a court-imposed judgment such as an unpaid tax or debt.

Line of Credit: The instrument of credit issued by a bank for short-term (one-year) capital needs. Most lines are revolving, meaning they can be drawn down, repaid, and drawn down again.

LTV (Loan-to-Value): The correlation between the actual amount borrowed on a loan and the value of the property.

Mechanic's Lien: A lien placed on a property by a contractor, usually because of nonpayment.

Mentor: Someone who has experience and expertise in a field and is willing to teach those who aspire to it. May be a paid professional program or an informal relationship.

MLS (Multiple Listing Service): A service used by real estate agents to list the properties they have for sale.

Mortgage: A legal document that pledges property to a lender as security for the repayment of the loan. The term also is used to refer to the loan itself.

Mortgage Broker: An independent professional who specializes in bringing together borrowers and lenders to facilitate real estate mortgages.

Note: The actual document of a debt, which includes the amount, interest rate, maturity dates, and the names of the parties obligated to pay. Notes may be sold or assigned to a third party.

Option: An agreement that gives the buyer a certain amount of time to purchase a property. Obligates the seller to sell the property, but does not obligate the buyer to purchase the property.

Overfinancing: Placing a mortgage on a property for more than the property is actually worth.

Owner Finance: Financing provided by the seller of a property. No bank qualifying.

Payoff Letter: A letter from a mortgage lender or other creditor that details the balance of a mortgage or debt.

PITI: Principal, interest, taxes, and insurance combined to make up a mortgage payment.

Point: A fee that equals 1 percent of the amount of a loan.

Prepayment Clause: The portion of a contract that describes the charge a lender collects when/if a borrower pays off the loan before the original payoff date.

Proration: The division of expense between buyer and seller to account for payment of an expense which exceeds ownership.

Refinance: Obtaining a new mortgage loan to pay off all or part of an existing mortgage loan.

Rent-to-Own: An agreement that allows an individual to rent a property with the intention of obtaining financing to purchase the property within a predetermined amount of time.

Retailing: The purchase of property for the purpose of renovating it to be sold to a user at full value.

Second Mortgage: A mortgage that has a second lien behind the primary mortgage.

Section 8: A government program underwritten by HUD and administrated locally that allows low-income families to choose and lease affordable, privately owned rental housing.

Secured Loan: A loan that has tangible assets such as property pledged as collateral for the loan. Mortgages are all secured loans.

Split Funding: A deal that an investor funds at two different times. A down payment is usually required, and another date is set for another payment.

Survey: The blueprint or map showing the boundaries of a property.

Tax Sale: A sale conducted by local taxing authorities to recover unpaid taxes.

Title: The right to, and the ownership of, land by the owner. Title is sometimes used to mean the evidence or proof of ownership of land; another term used for proof of ownership is "deed."

Title Company: A company that handles closings and title searches.

Title Insurance: Coverage that protects lenders and homeowners against loss of their interest in a property because of legal problems with the title.

Title Search: A check of the title records to ensure that the seller is the legal owner of the property and that no liens or other claims are outstanding.

Transfer Tax: A state or local tax that is paid when property ownership is transferred from one person to another.

Trustee: The individual or entity controlling the rights to a property held in trust for another entity.

Unsecured Loan: A loan that does not have any underlying collateral pledged to the lender. Rates for these types of loans are generally higher.

Variable Rate: The interest rate is not fixed at the time the loan is written; it goes up or down depending on the prime rate or some other stated rate of interest.

Warranty Deed: A deed issued by the seller that includes a guarantee that the title is clear and marketable.

Wholesaling: Purchasing undervalued properties and selling them to another investor at below market value for quick profit.

APPENDIX

BEGINNER'S TOOL KIT

APPENDIX I

LANDLORDING

RENTAL APPLICATION

Prospective Addresses _____

Desired Date of Occupancy _____

Desired Length of Occupancy _____

Smoke? ____ Yes ____ No   Type of Pets _____

TENANT NAME _____

Phone No(s) _____

Social Security #_____   Date of Birth _____

Street, City, Zip _____

Monthly Income   Source: ___ Wages   ___ Support

___ Other (specify) _____

Monthly Take-Home Pay _____

Employer's Name _____

Address _____

Phone _____   Supervisor _____

Your Position _____   How Long? _____

Previous Employer _____   Phone _____

Driver's License # _____   State _____

Car Make _____   Model _____   Year _____

Car License #_____   State ____   Monthly Payment_____

SPOUSE _____ Social Security # _____

Monthly Take-Home Pay _____

Employer's Name _____

Address _____

Phone _____ Supervisor _____

Your Position _____ How Long? _____

Previous Employer _____ Phone _____

Driver's License # _____ State _____

OTHER TENANTS   Relationship   Age/Occupation

_____

_____

_____

Why are you moving from your current home? _____

Current Landlord Name _____ Phone _____

Address_____ How Long? _____

Previous Street, City, Zip _____

Previous Landlord Name _____ Phone _____

CREDIT REFERENCES   Address   Limit   Good Standing?

1 _____

2. _____

3 _____

4. _____

BANK REFERENCES

Branch _____ Account # _____

Checking/Savings/Loan _____

PERSONAL REFERENCES

	Address	Phone	How Known/No. Yrs.

1. _____

2. _____

3. _____

NEAREST RELATIVE _____

Address _____

Phone _____ How Related? _____

Do you own any real estate? ___ yes ___ no

  If so, where and what? _____

Do you pay rent and bills on time? ___ yes ___ no

  If not, explain: _____

Do you know of anything that may interrupt income or rent?

___ yes ___ no

Have you ever been evicted from any tenancy? ___ yes ___ no

I hereby certify that the answers I have given in this application are true and correct to the best of my knowledge. I authorize a credit report to be completed for the purpose of credit verification.

Tenant _____ Date _____

Spouse _____ Date _____

SECTION 8 NOTICE

Request for Tenancy Approval
Housing Choice Voucher Program

Public reporting burden for this collection of information is estimated to average 5 minutes per response, including the time for reviewing instructions, searching existing data sources, gathering and maintaining the data needed, and completing and reviewing the collection of information. This agency may not conduct or sponsor, and a person is not required to respond to, a collection of information unless that collection displays a valid OMB control number.

Eligible families submit this information to the Public Housing Authority (PHA) when applying for housing assistance under Section 8 of the U.S. Housing Act of 1937 (42 U.S.C. 14371). The PHA uses the information to determine if the family is eligible, if the unit is eligible, and if the lease complies with program and statutory requirements. Responses are required to obtain a benefit from the Federal Government. The information requested does not lend itself to confidentiality.

---

1. Name of Public Housing Agency (PHA   2. Address of Unit (street, apartment number, city, state, zip)

HOUSING AUTHORITY CITY OF PITTSBURGH
200 Ross Street, Pittsburgh, PA 15219

---

3. Requested Beginning Date of Lease	4. Number of Bedrooms	5. Year Constructed	6. Proposed Rent	7. Security Deposit Amt.	8. Date available for inspection

---

9. Type of House/Apartment

___ Single Family Detached ___ Semi-Detached/Row House ___ Manufactured Home ___ Garden/Walkup
___ Elevator/High-Rise

---

10. If this unit is subsidized, indicate type of subsidy:

___ Section 202 ___ Section 221(d)(3)(BMIR) ___ Section 236 (insured or noninsured)
___ Section 515 Rural Development

---

11. Utilities and Appliances

The owner shall provide or pay for the utilities and appliances indicated below by an "O". The tenant shall provide or pay for the utilities and appliances indicated below by a "T". Unless otherwise specified below, the owner shall pay for all utilities and appliances provided by the owner.

Item	Specify fuel type				Provided by	Paid by
Heating	___ Natural gas	___ Bottle gas	___ Oil or electric	___ Coal or other		
Cooking	___ Natural gas	___ Bottle gas	___ Oil or electric	___ Coal or other		
Water heating	___ Natural gas	___ Bottle gas	___ Oil or electric	___ Coal or other		
Other Electric						
Water						
Sewer						

Trash Collection

_____

Air Conditioning

_____

Refrigerator

_____

Range/Microwave

_____

Other (Specify)

_____

NOTE: Prior to approval of this assisted tenancy, the owner or agent is required to supply proof of ownership of site control that is acceptable to the Housing Authority. Such acceptable proof may include a deed, land contract or purchase agreement.

12. Owner's Certifications. By executing this request, the owner certifies that:

   a. The most recent rent charged for the above unit was $_____ per month. The rent included the following utilities:

The reason for any differences between the prior rent and the proposed rent in Bloc 6 is:

   b. The owner (including a principal or other interested party) is not the parent, child, grandparent, grandchild, sister or brother of any member of the family, unless the PHA has determined (and has notified the owner and the family of such determination) that approving rental of the unit, notwithstanding such relationship, would provide reasonable accommodation for a family member who is a person with disabilities.

   _____ The unit, common areas servicing the unit, and exterior painted surfaces associated with such unit or common areas have been found to be lead-based paint free by a lead-based paint inspector certified under the Federal certification program or under a federally accredited State or Tribal certification program.

   _____ A completed statement is attached containing disclosure of known information on lead-based paint and/or lead-based paint hazards in the unit, common areas or exterior painted surfaces, including a statement that the owner has provided the lead hazard information pamphlet to the family.

13. PHA Determinations

   a. The PHA has not screened the family's behavior or suitability for tenancy. Such screening is the owner's own responsibility.

   b. The owner's lease must include word-for-word all provisions of the HUD tenancy addendum.

   c. The PHA will arrange for inspection of the unit and will notify the owner and family as to whether or not the unit will be approved.

_____

Print or Type Name of Owner or Other Party Authorized to Execute Lease   Print or Type Name of Family

_____

Signature   Signature

_____

Business Address   Present address of family
                                                   (Street, apartment no., city, state & zip code)

_____

Telephone Number   Date mm/dd/yy   Telephone Number   Date mm/dd/yy

OWNER CERTIFICATION
Payment of Real Estate Taxes and Other Assessments

Property:
(Please list address of the property requested for approval)

_____

_____

COMPLETE THE SECTION THAT APPLIES:

1. Certification of Payment
    (Owner's certification of no outstanding payments due)

I, _____(print name),
hereby certify that for the above described property, as of this date, I do
not owe any over-due payment for real estate taxes to the City of
Pittsburgh, or the County of Allegheny; nor do I owe any outstanding
amounts to the Pittsburgh Water & Sewer Authority or ALCOSAN.

_____   _____

Signature   Date

2. Certification of Approved Payment Plan
    (Owner's certification of approved payment plan)

I, _____(print name),
hereby certify that for the above described property, as of this date, I do
not owe any over-due payment for real estate taxes to the City of
Pittsburgh, or the County of Allegheny; nor do I owe any outstanding
amounts to the Pittsburgh Water & Sewer Authority or ALCOSAN,
EXCEPT that I have entered into a payment plan approved by the
proper authority(ies) for the following taxing body(ies) and/or municipal
utility entity(ies) (list all that apply):

_____

_____

_____   _____

Signature   Date

Disclosure of Information on Lead-Based Paint and/or Lead-Based Paint Hazards

Lead Warning Statement
Housing built before 1978 may contain lead-based paint. Lead from paint, paint chips, and dust can pose health hazards if not managed properly. Lead exposure is especially harmful to young children and pregnant women. Before renting pre-1978 housing, lessors must disclose the presence of known lead-based paint and/or lead-based paint hazards in the dwelling. Lessees must also receive a federally approved pamphlet on lead poisoning prevention.

Lessor's Disclosure
(a)   Presence of lead-based paint and/or lead-based paint hazards (check (i) or (ii) below):
  (i)____ Known lead-based paint and/or lead-based paint hazards are present in the housing (explain)

_____

_____

  (ii)____ Lessor has no knowledge of lead-based paint and/or lead-based paint hazards in the housing.
(b)   Records and reports available to the lessor (check (i) or (ii) below):
  (i)____ Lessor has provided the lessee with all available records and reports pertaining to lead-based paint and/or lead-based paint hazards in the housing (list documents below):

_____

_____

  (ii)____ Lessor has no reports or records pertaining to lead-based paint and/or lead-based paint hazards in the housing.

Lessee's Acknowledgment
(c)_____ Lessee has received copies of all information listed above.

(d)_____ Lessee has received the pamphlet *Protect Your Family from Lead in Your Home*

Agent's Acknowledgment (initial)
(e)_____ Agent has informed the lessor of the lessor's obligations under 42 U.S.C. 4852(d) and is aware of his/her responsibility to ensure compliance.

Certification of Accuracy
The following parties have reviewed the information above and certify, to the best of their knowledge, that the information they have provided is true and accurate.

Lessor	Date	Lessor	Date
Lessor	Date	Lessor	Date
Lessor	Date	Agent	Date

SECTION 8
LEASE AGREEMENT

This agreement dated_____is by and between
_____hereinafter called "Lessor" and
_____hereinafter called "Tenant" for the
unit located at _____

Under the following conditions:

1. TERM

    1. The initial term of this agreement shall be for _____
        (11-1/2) MONTHS beginning on _____
        and ending on _____
        for the total sum of $ _____

    2. Upon the expiration of the initial term, this agreement shall
        automatically renew for successive month-to-month terms.

2. RENTAL PAYMENT

    1. The tenant shall pay the Lessor as rent for the leased premises
        in monthly installments in advance without demand
        at _____
    2. From the beginning of the term the sum of $_____, in
        advance thereafter during the term of any renewal thereof, until
        the whole amount of said rent is paid.

3. UTILITIES AND APPLIANCES

    1. The landlord shall provide the utilities listed in the column below
        for the dwelling unit without any additional charge to the Tenant.
        The cost of these utilities is included in the contract rent. The
        utilities listed in the column below that are not included in the
        contract rent are to be paid by the tenant.

Utility	Type	Owner/Tenant Responsible
Heating	Natural Gas	Tenant
Cooking Heat	Natural Gas	Tenant
Lights		Tenant
Water Heating	Natural Gas	Tenant

Water	Owner
Sewage	Owner
Other	Tenant

b. 1) The range for the dwelling unit shall be provided by the <u>TENANT</u> (specify Landlord or Tenant, unspecified shall be provided by Landlord).

b. 2) The refrigerator for the dwelling unit shall be provided by the <u>TENANT</u> (specify Landlord or Tenant, unspecified shall be provided by Landlord).

4.   LESSOR RESPONSIBILITIES

The Lessor shall:

1. Comply with all State, County and/or Municipal Building, Fire Prevention, Housing and Health Department Codes applicable to the Lessor.

2. Maintain the unit in accordance with Housing Quality Standards (HQS), including performance of ordinary and extraordinary maintenance, unless otherwise stated in Additional Provisions section of this lease.

5. TENANT RESPONSIBILITIES

The Tenant shall:

1. Comply with all State, County, and/or Municipal Building, Fire Prevention, Housing and Health Department codes applicable to the tenant.

2. Maintain and keep the premises during the term in good repair and agree to pay for repairs of any damages they or their guests have caused.

3. Make no additions or alternations without prior consent of the lessor.

4. Not sublet any part of the premises nor assign this agreement to anyone else.

5. Not lawfully occupy the premises after the end of the term. If the tenant continues to occupy the premises after the end of the term, the tenant shall be directly responsible for all rent due and payable to the Owner of the premises.

6. SECURITY DEPOSIT

    The tenant has paid a security deposit in the amount of $_____ to the Lessor, for damages, unpaid rent and/or any other charges due under the lease.

7. ADDITIONAL PROVISIONS (IF ANY)

    N/A

8. LEASE ADDENDUM

    The attached Lease Addendum and Prohibited Lease Provisions are incorporated herein and made a part of this lease.

ACKNOWLEDGMENT

All parties hereby acknowledge that they have read this Agreement and understand it and agree to it.

WITNESS:

_____(Seal)
(Lessor)

_____(Seal)
(Date)

_____(Seal)
(Tenant)

_____(Seal)
(Date)

STANDARD LEASE AGREEMENT

This is a residential lease. It is a legally binding contract between the Landlord and each Tenant. Each Tenant should read this lease carefully.

The residential lease contains waivers of your right as a Tenant. Each Tenant should not sign this lease until each Tenant understands all of the agreements in this lease.

1. NAMES OF LANDLORD AND TENANT
    Name of the Landlord:
    Name(s) of the Tenant(s):
    LEASED PREMISES:
    The leased premises is the place that Landlord agrees to lease to Tenant. The leased premises:

2. STARTING AND ENDING DATES OF LEASE AGREEMENT
    This lease begins on:
    This lease ends on:
    The amount of rent is $ _____ per month

    Tenant agrees to pay the monthly rent in advance on or before the 1st day of each month. Landlord does not have to ask (MAKE DEMAND UPON) Tenant to pay the rent. Tenant agrees to pay rent by first class mail postage prepaid or in person to Landlord at the place specified by the Landlord.

    Tenant agrees to pay a LATE CHARGE of $ _____ if Tenant does not pay the rent by the 5th day of the month. The late charge fee shall not give the Tenant the right to further delay the rental installment, due and payable, beyond the late charge date. If Tenant mails the rent to the Landlord, at_____, the date of payment will be the date the letter is postmarked.

3. SECURITY DEPOSIT

    Tenant agrees to pay a security deposit of $_____. Tenant agrees to pay the security deposit to Landlord before the lease starts and before Landlord gives possession of the leased premises to Tenant.

    Landlord can take money from the security deposit to pay for any damages caused by Tenant, Tenant's family and Tenant's guests. Landlord may take the security deposit to pay for any unpaid rent.

After deducting for damages and unpaid rent, Landlord agrees to send the Tenant any security deposit money that remains. Landlord will send the remaining security deposit money to Tenant no later than 30 days after the lease expires and Tenant leaves. Landlord also agrees to send Tenant a written list of damages and amount deducted from the security deposit.

Tenant agrees to give Landlord a written forwarding address when he vacates and the lease expires.

Tenant may not use the security deposit as payment of the final month's rent.

Tenant agrees that Landlord is not responsible to Tenant, Tenant's family or guests for damage or injury caused by water, snow, or ice that comes on the leased premises unless the Landlord was negligent.

4. KEY DEPOSIT

Tenant agrees to pay a key deposit of $_____. Landlord agrees to send the Tenant the key deposit upon return of keys at end of the lease.

5. LANDLORD'S DUTY AT THE BEGINNING OF LEASE

Landlord agrees to give Tenant possession of the leased premises on the beginning date of the lease. The lease will begin even if Landlord cannot give Tenant possession of the leased premises because the prior Tenant is still in the leased premises or the leased premises is damaged. IF LANDLORD CANNOT GIVE TENANT POSSESSION, TENANT DOES NOT HAVE TO PAY RENT UNTIL THE DAY POSSESSION OF THE LEASED PREMISES IS GIVEN TO TENANT.

6. DAMAGE TO LEASED PREMISES

Tenant agrees to notify Landlord immediately if the leased premises are damaged by fire or any other cause. Tenant agrees to notify Landlord if there is any condition in the leased premises that could damage the leased premises or harm Tenants or others. If Tenant cannot live in the entire leased premises because of damage or destroy, Tenant may:

a) Live in the undamaged portion of the leased premises and pay less rent until the leased premises is repaired, or

b) Terminate the lease and vacate the leased premises.

Tenant agrees that if the leased premises is damaged or destroyed and Tenant terminates the lease, Landlord has no further responsibility to Tenant.

7. INSURANCE

Landlord agrees to carry insurance on the building where the leased premises is located. The Tenant's own personal property is not insured under the Landlord's insurance. Tenant is responsible for Tenant's own property that is located in the leased premises.

8. ASSIGNMENTS OR SUBLEASE BY TENANTS

Assignment (or Assign) is the legal terminology for a transfer of the lease from the Tenant to another individual. This other individual then becomes the Landlord's new Tenant and takes over the lease.

Tenant agrees not to transfer (assign) this lease to anyone without written consent of Landlord.

A sublease is a separate lease between the Tenant and another person who leases all or part of leased premise from the Tenant.

Tenant agrees not to lease (sublease) all or any part of the lease premises to anyone else without the written consent of Landlord. Tenant agrees that if Tenant transfers this lease (assigns) or leases all or part of the leased premises to another (sublease), Tenant has violated this lease.

9. RESPONSIBILITY FOR DAMAGE TO PROPERTY OR INJURY TO PEOPLE

Landlord is responsible for all damage to property or injury to people caused by Landlord or Landlord's representative (intentional or negligent acts at the leased premises). Tenant is responsible for all damage to the leased premises and injury to people caused by Tenant, Tenant's family or guests.

Tenant agrees that Landlord is not responsible to Tenant, Tenant's family or guests for damage or injury caused by water, snow, or ice that comes on the leased premises unless the Landlord was negligent.

10. USE OF LEASED PREMISES

Tenant agrees to use the leased premises only as a residence. Tenant agrees to obey all federal, state, and local laws and regulations when using the leased premises. Tenant agrees not to store any flammable, hazardous or toxic chemicals or substances in or around the leased premises.

Tenant agrees not to perform any activities in or around the leased premises which could harm anyone or damage any property.

Tenant agrees that Tenant will not allow more than _____ to occupy the leased premises without the written permission of Landlord. Any other person occupying premises is a breach of this agreement. There is an additional seventy-five ($75.00) per month charge for each additional person.

11. RULES AND REGULATIONS

Tenant agrees to obey all rules and regulations for the leased premises. If Tenant violates any of the rules and regulations for the leased premises, then the Tenant has violated this lease.

12. LANDLORD'S RIGHT TO MORTGAGE THE LEASED PREMISES (SUBORDINATION)

Subordinate and subordination are legal terms that mean that this lease does not have any effect upon the rights of the Landlord's mortgage company. In other words, Tenant's rights under this lease are subordinate to Landlord's mortgage company. If Landlord does not make the mortgage payments, the mortgage company may have the right to terminate the Landlord's ownership of the leased premises. If the mortgage company sells the leased premises at a mortgage foreclosure sale, the lease may be terminated.

Tenant agrees that the Landlord has the right to mortgage the leased premises. If Landlord has a mortgage on the leased premises now, or if Landlord gets a mortgage in the future, Tenant agrees that this lease is subordinate to the Landlord's mortgage.

13. CARE OF LEASED PREMISES

Tenant is responsible for, and will take care of, the leased premises and all of the property in and around the leased premises. Tenant agrees to pay for any damage caused by Tenant, Tenant's family and Tenant's guests. Tenant agrees to vacate the leased premises to Landlord when the lease ends.

14. LANDLORD'S RIGHT TO ENTER LEASED PREMISES

Tenant agrees that Landlord or Landlord's representatives have the right to enter the leased premises at reasonable times. Landlord and Landlord's representatives have the right to inspect, to make repairs, to do maintenance, and to show the leased premises to others.

15. UTILITY SERVICES

Landlord and Tenant agree to pay charges for utilities and services supplied to the leased premises as follows:

UTILITY	RESPONSIBLE PARTY
Television Cable	
Electric to Premises	
Water Service	
Gas Service	
Refuse Collection	
Lawn Maintenance	
Snow and Leaf Removal	
Water Softener Charges	
Sewer Charges	
Condominium Fee	
Homeowner's Association fee	
Parking Fee	
Pest Control Charges	
Other—Appliances	
Other—	

Landlord has the right to turn off any utility temporarily or other service to the leased premises in order to make repairs or do maintenance.

16. GOVERNMENTAL POWER OF EMINENT DOMAIN

Eminent domain is the legal name for the right of a governmental entity such as the state or county or city to take private property for public use. The government must pay fair compensation to anyone who has any right in the property that is taken by the government.

If all or any part of the leased premises (or the building within which the leased premises is located) is taken by eminent domain, this lease will end automatically. Landlord and Tenant agree to release each other from any responsibility because leased premises is taken by eminent domain and the lease had ended.

17. VIOLATIONS OF THIS LEASE

If the Landlord or Tenant does not fulfill anything that has been agreed upon, it is a violation of this lease. If Tenant violates this lease, Tenants may lose their security deposit. If Tenant violates this lease, Landlord also can take legal steps towards the Tenant for other expenses and may legally evict tenant.

<u>Each Tenant should not sign this lease unless each Tenant has read and clearly understands the information in this section regarding lease violations.</u>

_____ THIS IS A JOINT AND SEVERAL LEASE

_____ THIS IS NOT A JOINT AND SEVERAL LEASE

If this is NOT a joint and several lease, then the Landlord can only sue one Tenant's violation of the lease.

If this is a joint and several lease, it means that all the Tenants as a group and each of the Tenants as an individual are responsible to Landlord for all of the agreements of this lease. For example, if the rent is not paid, Landlord can sue ALL Tenants (jointly) for any unpaid rent, or Landlord can bring a suit against any one Tenant separately (severally) for all of the unpaid rent.

TENANT VIOLATES THIS LEASE IF TENANT:

a)   Fails to pay rent or other charges to Landlord on time.

b) Leaves (abandons the lease premises without the Landlord's permission before the end of the lease).

c) Does not leave the leased premises at the end of the lease.

d) Does not do all of the things that Tenant agreed to do in this lease.

If Tenant violates the lease, each Tenant agrees to waive notice to quit. This means that the Landlord may file a complaint in court asking for an order evicting each Tenant from the leased premises without giving each Tenant notice to quit first. Landlord does not have the right to throw Tenant out of the leased premises (self-help eviction). The Landlord can only evict Tenant by court action.

The Landlord does not have the right to sue in court for eviction unless a Tenant has violated the agreements in this lease. Even though each Tenant is waiving notice to quit, each Tenant will have a chance in court to challenge the Landlord's claim for eviction.

If Tenant violates the lease agreement, the Landlord may sue each Tenant in court:

e) To collect overdue rent, late charges and money damages caused by Tenant's violation of the agreement in the lease.

f) To recover possession of the leased premises (eviction).

g) To collect for unpaid rent until the end of the lease or until another person takes possession of the leased premises as a new Tenant.

Tenant agrees that Landlord may receive reasonable attorney fees as part of a court judgment in a lawsuit against Tenant for violation of the agreements of the lease.

a) Landlord and Tenant agree that the additional agreements marked with a "yes" are part of this lease agreement.

Yes __X__ No. _____ Check-In and Check-Out Procedures
Yes __X__ No. _____ Rules and Regulations
Yes __X__ No. _____ Tenant's Right to Continue Lease
Yes __X__ No. _____ No Pet Agreement
Yes __X__ No. _____ Single Family Residence Agreement
Yes _____ No. _____ Other

b) Tenant will use a charcoal or flammable gas grill in the leased premises or on any balcony, patio, or other common area on the property as long as it is used in a safe manner upon which the leased premises is located.

c) No window treatments, awnings, draperies or umbrellas will be installed in the leased premises without the prior written consent of Landlord.

d) Tenant will observe "quiet hours" between the hours of 11:00 p.m. and 8:00 a.m. daily.

e) Tenant, Tenant's family members, Tenant's guest or invitee will not disturb any other resident of the building in which the leased premises is located in any way.

f) There will be no waterbeds within the leased premises.

g) Tenant will not install shelving, picture hooks, wallpaper, paint or alter in any way in the future of the leased premises without the prior written consent of the Landlord.

h) Tenant will be responsible for testing all fire warning devices such as smoke detectors and fire alarms within the leased premises and will notify Landlord if any fire warning or fire abatement device is not functional. Tenant will not disable, or permit to be disabled, any fire warning or discharge any fire extinguisher.

i) Tenant will not go upon the roof of the building within which the leased premises are located and will not enter any area clearly designated as being closed to Tenants and others.

j) Tenant will not permit the premises to be unoccupied for longer than five (5) consecutive days without notifying the Landlord.

k) Tenant will not permit any person(s), except for person(s) provided for in the Agreement, to occupy the leased premises for longer than five (5) consecutive days without notifying the Landlord.

l) There will be NO alcoholic beverages consumed in the common area of the building and grounds within which the leased premises is located.

m) Tenant will keep the leased premises clean and dispose of all rubbish, garbage and other waste in a clean and safe manner.

n) Tenant will at all times be in compliance with any recycling programs.

o) Tenant will provide a telephone number for both the leased premises and their place of business to Landlord.

p) Tenant will be responsible for setting garbage out on the curb no sooner than one day before pick-up.

q) Tenant will only use off-white paint in the leased premises with the Landlord's consent.

r) Tenant will not paint any unpainted woodwork in the leased premises.

s) Tenant will not have or permit to have in the leased premises any type of tank which holds more than five (5) gallons of water.

BY SIGNING THIS LEASE AGREEMENT, EACH TENANT AGREES THAT HE/SHE HAS READ AND UNDERSTANDS ALL OF THE TERMS IN THIS LEASE AND AGREES TO BE BOUND BY ITS TERMS.

OWNER NAME:

TENANT NAME:

RENT AMOUNT:

PROPERTY ADDRESS:

_____   _____
Landlord's Signature   Date

_____   _____
Tenant's Signature   Date

_____   _____
Tenant's Signature   Date

TENANT'S RIGHT TO CONTINUE LEASE

LANDLORD:

TENANT:

PREMISES:

LEASE:

START DATE:

END DATE:

Landlord agrees that Tenant has the right to continue this lease for 12 months after the ending date of the lease. If Tenant wants to continue the lease for 12 months, Tenant must notify Landlord in writing. Tenant must notify Landlord in writing no later than _____.

1.   Landlord agrees that Tenant has the right to continue this lease only if Tenant has not violated the lease.

2.   Tenant agrees to pay a new monthly rental of $_____ per month beginning _____

3.   If Tenant continues this lease, Landlord and Tenant agree that all of the agreements of the lease are the same and will continue. The lease amount and ending date will be modified as follows:

> New monthly rental amount: $
> New lease ending date:
> Landlord and Tenant agree that "TENANT'S RIGHT TO CONTINUE LEASE" is a part of the lease between Landlord and Tenant.

Landlord's Signature	Date
Tenant's Signature	Date
Tenant's Signature	Date

TENANT MOVE-IN CHECKLIST

Address_____ Tenant _____

Dates

Application filled out and fee collected   _____

Verification forms signed   _____

Deposit given to reserve rental   _____

First month's rent collected   _____

Security deposit collected   _____

Move-in payment schedule needed   _____

Rental agreement signed and explained   _____

    Additional agreements   _____   _____

                                    _____   _____

                                    _____   _____

Information sheet for new tenants given   _____

On-time payments emphasized/collection procedures   _____

Rental inventory sheet given and checked   _____

Office hours/maintenance request/repair policies explained _____

Periodic inspections discussed   _____

Renter's insurance suggested   _____

_____   _____

_____   _____

RENTER'S INSURANCE NOTICE

From: Houses Unlimited, Inc.

3049 Chartiers Avenue

Pittsburgh, PA 15204

To: Tenant

Dear New Tenant:

Our insurance, like other standard rental policies, covers only the building itself against fire. Standard rental policies do not cover your personal belongings against damage or theft. It is your responsibility to make sure you have provisions for coverage of your own possessions. You might not think you need it, but there may come a time when something will happen that you do.

If you do not have an insurance agent, we have insurance agents available to help you at your own cost.

Thank you,

S. Timmerson

HOUSES UNLIMITED, INC.

MANAGEMENT AGREEMENT

Agreement between_____

owner(s) and _____

manager(s), for management of the properties located at _____

_____

Compensation for manager(s) shall be $_____ per hours worked with a guaranteed weekly minimum of _____ hours. Work will not exceed _____ hours weekly without the owner's consent, unless to handle an emergency. Additional compensation or bonuses shall be as follows:

_____

_____

Duties include:

1. Meet or call owner weekly (or monthly) to consult on the job priorities and give updated reports on the properties.

2. Submit weekly time sheets to the owner detailing: daily activities, number of hours worked, materials purchased and receipts.

3. Provide his or her phone number to tenants so they will have an emergency number to call. Within reason, manager should be able to respond at any time to an emergency.

4. Schedule his or her own work week and days off based on week's activities. Manager will keep the following day(s) available as a regular day for routine maintenance _____

5. Schedule appointments for showing vacancies and accept applications and initial deposits.

6. Be responsible for decisions related to needed repairs, consulting with the owner on major projects or purchases.

7.   Other duties include: _____

_____

Either manager or owner may cancel this agreement at any time after
giving _____ days notice to the other party.

Dated: _____

Manager(s) _____

Owner(s)_____ By _____

MANAGEMENT AGREEMENT

MACE PROPERTY MANAGEMENT
811 Washington Avenue
Carnegie, PA 15106
(412) 279-0519

This agreement made this _____ day of _____,
20____, by and between_____
(Hereinafter referred to as "Owner") and Mace Property Management
(Hereinafter referred to as "Agent").

1. Appointment and Acceptance: Owner hereby appoints Agent as
    sole and exclusive Agent of Owner to lease and manage the
    property described in paragraph 2, upon the terms and conditions
    provided herein. Agent accepts the appointment and agrees to
    furnish the services of its organization for the leasing and
    management of the rental property, and Owner agrees to pay all
    expenses in connection with those services.

2. Description of Rental Property: The property to be managed by
    agent under this agreement is located at/known as_____
    _____herein referred to as the "Rental
    Property".

3. Term: This Agreement shall become effective on_____
    and shall continue in full force and effect for a minimum of (1) year
    from the effective date. Thereafter, it shall continue in full force and
    effect unless either party shall serve written notice of cancellation
    sent by certified mail to the other party, in which event this
    Agreement shall terminate sixty (60) days after the service of such
    notice. If, however, this agreement is terminated while a lease(s), or
    subsequent lease renewal(s) of the Rental Property is (are) still in
    effect or as long as tenant remains in the property under any
    circumstances, Owner shall pay agent all management fees that
    owner would have been obligated to pay if this agreement had not
    been terminated, until the expiration of said lease(s) or subsequent
    lease renewal(s) of the rental property, so long as said tenant(s) was
    (were) originally procured and placed into the Rental Property by
    Agent.

4. Initial Deposit and Contingency Reserve: Immediately upon
    commencement of this agreement, Owner shall remit to agent the
    sum of $_____ as an initial deposit representing the

estimated disbursements to be made the first month following the commencement of the agreement, plus an additional sum of $_____ as a contingency reserve. Owner agrees to maintain the amount of the contingency reserve stated above at all times to enable Agent to pay the obligations of Owner under this agreement as they become due. The amount of the contingency reserve may only be modified if such modification is in writing signed by Owner and Agent.

5. Leasing Vacant Space: Agent shall use all reasonable efforts to lease Rental Property to desirable tenants. Agent is authorized to advertise the Rental property or portions therefore for rent, using periodicals, signs, plans, brochures, or displays, or such other means as Agent may deem proper and advisable. Agent is authorized to place signs on the Rental Property advertising the Rental property for rent, provided such signs comply with applicable laws. At the discretion of the Agent, the cost (or portion thereof) of such advertising shall be paid by the Owner, such costs, if applicable, being deducted from the Owner's rental proceeds. Agent is authorized to negotiate, prepare, and execute all leases, including all renewals and extensions of leases and to cancel and modify existing lease, whether procured by Agent or Owner. All costs of leasing shall be borne by Owner.

6. Collection and Remittance of Income: The Agent is authorized to collect rents and other income from the Rental property promptly when such amounts become due and shall deposit all amounts so collected in a bank account maintained by the Agent. The Agent may withdraw from such bank account all disbursements which under this agreement are to be made at the expense of the Owner. Agent is further authorized to pay or reimburse itself for all other sums due Agent under this agreement, including Agent's compensation under paragraph 11 hereunder. In the event that the balance in an Owner's account is at any time insufficient to pay disbursements due and payable under this agreement, Owner shall immediately, upon notice, remit to Agent sufficient funds to cover the deficiency and replenish the contingency reserve (if applicable). In no event will Agent be required to use its own funds to pay such disbursements, nor shall Agent be required to advance any monies to or on behalf of the Owner. If Agents elect to advance any money in connection with the Rental Property to pay any expenses for Owner, such advance shall be considered a loan from Agent to Owner subject to repay with interest, and Owner hereby agrees to reimburse Agent including interest as provided in paragraph 11

hereunder and hereby authorizes Agent to deduct such amounts from any monies due Owner. The Agent shall submit to the Owner a monthly statement of receipts and disbursements; and, to the extent that funds are available (after maintaining the contingency reserve amount if applicable). Agent shall on a monthly basis pay to the Owner the Owner's share of the amounts in such accounts.

7. Security Deposits:

_____ The Agent shall hold all security deposits paid by tenants and shall retain all collected funds in an appropriate escrow account as per the Commonwealth of Pennsylvania Act of Assembly, No. 22 approved April 6, 1951, entitled "The Landlord and Tenant Act of 1951".

_____ The Owner shall hold all security deposits paid by tenants and shall retain all collected funds in an appropriate escrow account as per the Commonwealth of Pennsylvania Act of Assembly, No. 22 approved April 6, 1951, entitled "The Landlord and Tenant Act of 1951". In addition, Mace Property Management is held harmless of any recourse due to Owner's failure to return escrow deposit.

8. Maintenance and Operation:

Agent is authorized to make or cause to be made, through contracted services or otherwise, all ordinary repairs and replacements reasonably necessary to preserve the Rental Property in its present condition and for the operational efficiency of the Rental Property, and all alterations required to comply with lease requirements, Governmental regulations, or insurance requirements, provided the expense to be incurred for any one item of maintenance, alteration, refurbishing, or repair shall not exceed the sum of $_____, unless such expense is specifically authorized by the Owner, or is incurred under such circumstances as Agent shall reasonably deem to be an emergency where repairs are immediately necessary for the preservation and safety of the Rental Property, or to avoid the suspension of any essential service to the Rental Property, or to avoid danger to life or property, or to comply with federal, state, or local law, such emergency repairs shall be made by Agent at Owner's expense without prior approval. And Owner agrees to reimburse agent for such expenses. Agent is authorized to enter into agreements in Owner's name for all necessary repairs, maintenance, minor alterations, and utility services. Agent shall be authorized to make, in Owner's name and at Owner's expense, contracts on Owner's behalf for electricity, gas, fuel, or water, and such other services as Agent shall deem necessary or prudent for the operation of the Rental Property.

9. General Authority/Employees: Agent is authorized to perform all services, in addition to the forgoing, necessary for the management of the Rental Property. Such services shall include: to employ, discharge, supervise and pay on behalf of Owner, and at the expense of the Owner, all servants, employees, or contractors considered by the Agent as necessary for the maintenance and operation of the Rental Property, and to engage attorneys to commence, prosecute or defend any legal action which the Agent deems necessary to dispossess any tenant or other person from the Rental property, or to otherwise enforce any lease or contract or agreement executed by agent on behalf of Owner or to defend any action filed against Agent or Owner. The Agent shall not be liable to the Owner or to others for any act or omission on the part of such employees or attorneys if the Agent has taken reasonable care in their selection.

10. Attorney-In-Fact: Owner does hereby appoint Agent as its attorney-in-fact, and as such does hereby authorize said Agent to negotiate and execute on behalf of Owner all leases, extensions, renewals, or other contracts or agreements as Agent deems are reasonable and necessary for the management of the Rental Property, and to commence any and all legal actions as Agent deems necessary to enforce any lease, extension or renewal, or to evict any tenant, in the name of the Agent or Owner or to defend any action brought by any party against the Agent or Owner in connection therewith. Agent is authorized to engage counsel and to pay such fees and costs as may be necessary to enforce any lease extension or renewal or other contract or agreement executed by Agent on behalf of Owner in connection with the management of the Rental Property or to defend any action brought by any Party against Agent or Owner in connection therewith.

11. Compensation of Agent: The Owner shall pay the agent the following compensation:

a) For Management - _____% of the total gross monthly receipts from the Rental Property.

b) For Leasing - _____% of the first full month rental amount on all leases to new tenants secured by Agent or Owner.

c) For Renewal of Leases - $_____ will be charged for negotiation and preparation of a renewal of lease agreement, provided the same tenant occupies the Rental Property for a second term and any subsequent term.

d) For Extraordinary Services - If Agent is required or authorized to perform services not customarily a part of the usual services performed by a managing Agent, Owner shall pay agent additional compensation in an amount to be agreed upon between the parties. Such services include, but are not limited to: extraordinary repairs are made to the Rental Property; the Rental Property is reconstructed, modernized, rehabilitated; the Rental Property is restored after fire or other perils; supervision of general contracting, architectural, or engineering services; employing a collection agent for the purpose of collecting delinquent tenant charges.

e) Interest on any unpaid amounts due Agent under any provision of this agreement shall bear interest at the rate of _____% per annum.

f) For quarterly inspections $_____ of the interior of the leased premises.

g) For biannual inspections $_____ of the interior of the leased premises.

12. Agent's Liability/Indemnification: The Owner acknowledges and agrees that the Agent is acting as agent for Owner only in leasing and managing the Rental Property. Agent assumes the liability whatsoever for any acts or omissions of Owner, or any previous owners of Rental Property, or any previous management or other agent of either. Agent assumes no liability for any failure of or default by any tenant in the payment of any rent or other charges due Owner or in the performance of any obligations owed by any tenant to Owner pursuant to any lease or otherwise. Nor does Agent assume any liability for violations or any obligations or responsibilities of Owner with respect to the Rental Property under any environmental laws or regulations, including but not limited to any Lead Based Paint violations. Owner shall indemnify, defend, and save Agent harmless from all loss, causes of action, demands, debts, liability, damages, costs, expenses (including attorney's fee). In connection with agent's performance in good faith under this agreement, Owner shall further indemnify and save Agent harmless

and defend Agent from all liability or claim for personal injury or property damage incurred or occurring in, on or about the Rental Property or on the premises upon which the Rental Property is located. Owner's obligation to defend and indemnify Agent hereunder survives the termination of this agreement.

13. Insurance: Owner shall keep in force adequate insurance against physical damage (e.g., fire with extended coverage endorsement, boiler and machinery, etc.) and against liability for loss, damage, or injury to property or persons which might arise out of the occupancy, management, operation, or maintenance of the Rental Property. Agent shall be covered as an additional insured on all liability insurance maintained with respect to the Rental Property. Liability insurance shall be adequate to protect the interests of both the Owner and Agent and in form, substance, and amounts reasonably satisfactory to Agent. The amounts and types of insurance shall be acceptable to both the Owner and the Agent, and proof of all insurance shall be delivered by Owner to Agent in a form acceptable to the Agent.

14. Termination for Cause: Either Owner or Agent may terminate this agreement in the event of the dissolution, cessation of business (for any cause whatsoever), bankruptcy, insolvency, or assignments for the benefit of creditors of or by the other party. Owner shall give written notice to Agent within five (5) days of the occurrence of any of the foregoing events. In the event of a bona fide sale of Rental Property by Owner, either Owner or Agent may terminate this agreement upon the giving to the other at least thirty (30) days prior written notice by certified mail of such termination, effective if such sale is consummated. In addition either party may terminate in the event of any default by the other party of its obligations under this agreement for a continuous period of forty-five (45) days after written notice specifying the default and providing the opportunity within such period to cure the default. Any delays in performance of any obligation of Agent under this agreement shall be excused to the extent that such delays are caused by events not within the control of Agent, and any time periods required for performance shall be executed accordingly. Agent may assign its rights and delegate its duties under this agreement.

15. Non-Discrimination: Owner understands that in leasing the property, both Mace and Owner must fully comply with all laws and regulations of the Fair Housing Act which prohibits discrimination on the basis of race, color, creed, national origin, sex, handicap or familial status.

16. Sale of Property: If Owner sells the property to a tenant (or the spouse of such tenant) obtained by Mace, either during the term of the lease or thereafter, Owner will pay Mace as a commission _____% of the price for which the property is sold due to the fact that Mace would have been procuring cause of the sale.

17. Notices: Notice hereunder shall be valid if mailed to the agent at Mace Property Management, c/o Alex Deacon, P.O. Box 657, Carnegie, PA 15106.

I certify that I have read and understand this agreement.

_____   _____
Owner   Agent/Owner
                                                      Mace Property Management

_____   Owner

PAST DUE NOTICE

Houses Unlimited, Inc.

3049 Chartiers Avenue

Pittsburgh, PA 15204

412-777-3000

In Re: Past due rent

To: Tenant

    You are behind in your rental payments. I am enclosing a statement showing the current amount due and will expect you to send the amount you owe to the above address. Please make your check/money order payment to John Calhoun.

    Thank you for your cooperation in this matter.

Sincerely,

J. Timmerson
Houses Unlimited, Inc.

DEFERRED RENT AGREEMENT

Agreement to Pay Rent in Default

_____ (Tenant) hereby acknowledges that I
owe _____ to _____ (Landlord) which
represents past due rents. I agree to pay three payments of
_____ beginning 1/1/04 and continuing each 15 days
until this amount is paid in full. Any failure to pay will be cause for
immediate eviction.

_____ Tenant

_____ Date

Accepted by: _____ Landlord

_____ Date

NOTICE TO TERMINATE TENANCY

TO: Tenant

You are hereby required within 10 days from this date _____ to vacate, remove your belongings and deliver up possession of the premises, now held and used by you.

This eviction notice is the result of rent payment delinquency. We will not continue to carry arrears or delinquency in current month. You have signed a lease accepting responsibility of commitment. You are in non-compliance.

Should you fail to pay within the allotted time, legal proceedings will be instituted against you to recover possession, to declare said lease/rental forfeited, and to recover rents, damages, attorney fees and court costs for the period of the unlawful detention.

Please contact the office of the landlord/manager if you have questions regarding this notice.

Rental Manager: Houses Unlimited, Inc.

Telephone No. 412-777-3000

NOTICE TO VACATING TENANT

Dear Tenant:

We received notification that you will be vacating the house/apartment you now rent. We want to remind you that the property must be returned to us in the same condition it was given in order to receive your full security deposit back.

Return all keys to our office, because unless otherwise agreed on, you remain responsible for rent payment each day until the key is received by us.

After keys are received, we will make one final inspection to see if the property has been reasonably cleaned and without any damage. If all checks out well, your deposit will be refunded to you within 30 days. You must be sure to provide us with a forwarding address.

We have immediately begun advertising for new tenants. Let us know if you have any change of plans on your move date or know someone you can recommend, because we will be scheduling a new tenant to move in the day after you vacate. Also, if we can provide you with a larger rental or in another location better for you, let us know because we do have other rental units that will soon be available.

Thank you for your cooperation.

Sincerely,

Jackie Timmerson
Property Manager

Enclosure

SECURITY DEPOSIT REFUND REQUIREMENTS

From _____

_____

_____

Date _____

To _____

_____

Dear _____

To ensure you receive your full deposit, here is a checklist:

1. 30-day notices given
2. All walls, floors and ceilings thoroughly cleaned
3. All appliances cleaned (i.e., stove, oven, refrigerator)
4. Refrigerator unplugged and left open
5. All trash picked up and removed from house
6. Carpets must be cleaned
7. Any draperies and blinds, present at move in, must be hung back in place
8. All windows and doors closed and locked
9. Any damages to the property should be reported to our office at least 2 weeks before move out
10. All keys returned
11. Grass cut and raked

Deposit will be refunded within _____ days after you move to the forwarding address you must provide us.

Sincerely,

Rental Manager

VACANCY MAKEOVER CHECKLIST

_____ If drapes are provided, clean.

_____ Clean and check all appliances.

_____ Make sure all countertops, drawers, and cabinets are clean. Remove old shelf paper.

_____ Clean bathrooms, including tubs (remove any decals), toilets, tile on wall, tile on floor, mirror, medicine cabinets and vanities.

_____ Make sure bathroom details are in place and clean (towel bars, toilet paper holders, soap dishes).

_____ Clean and shine all vinyl floorings.

_____ Clean all windows and mirrors.

_____ Remove all debris or personal items left.

_____ Clean carpets.

APPENDIX II

RETAILING

MARKETING POSTCARDS AND ADS

Postcards

Houses Unlimited, Inc.
3049 Chartiers Avenue
Pittsburgh, PA 15204

WE BUY HOUSES!
Any Condition ★ Any Price Range ★ Any Area!

★★★★★★★★★★★
Sell Your Home
Within 9 Days!
★★★★★★★★★★★

A fast, easy and convenient way to sell your house

Interested in selling your house without paying thousands of dollars in real estate commissions? Concerned about agents having a key to your property and needing access all times of the day and evening? Would a quick sell help you out? This is for you.

Hundreds of our satisfied clients can tell you how easy it is to do business with Houses Unlimited. There are a number of reasons that property owners need a quick sale and close on their property and we are here to help. If you are moving out of the area, have responsibility for a vacant property or need to cash out or downscale your housing costs, **Houses Unlimited Inc.** can offer the solution to your problem. One call to us at (412)777-3000 is all it takes. We buy houses regularly and close within 30 days . . . cash in your hands when you need it.

Houses Unlimited Inc. is a private investment company—not a Realtor or a real estate company. We offer several unique ways which allow people like you to sell their houses without the time delays and hassles of traditional home selling. Best yet, we don't charge any fees or commissions at all. Call us today and see how we can help you.

Free! No Obligation Consultation, Call (412)777-3000

See our website @ www.housesunlimitedinc.com

Door Hangers

We Buy Houses

If you need cash or have been thinking
about selling your house...

Call us 412-777-3000

We are not real estate agents or
traders—we are investors

We Pay for Referrals

Business Cards

Real Estate Investment
Buy ★ Sell ★ Rent

Joe Investor
555-1212

We will buy your home and you get the cash
in days—any condition.

Cash for Your Home
Property Vacant?
Need Repairs?
Behind on the Mortgage?
Need the Cash for Any Reason?

Call us ★ We can help
555-1212

Newspaper Classifieds

NEED CASH?
We'll buy your house
& close quickly
555-1212

Properties Wanted
Any area—Any condition
Call us for an offer
Immediate Closing 555-1212

Investors Seek House
Any Condition
We can make you an offer immediately
Fast Closing 555-1212

PROPERTY INFORMATION SHEET

Property Address: _____ Area (circle one) Good Fair Bad

Owner Name: _____ Phone: _____

Vacant: (circle one)   Yes   No

Construction: (circle one)   Brick   Frame   Other

No. of Bedrooms: _____ No. of Bathrooms: _____

Asking Price: $ _____

After Repair Value

(ARV): $ _____

Est. Repair Amt. $ _____

Maximum Offer $ _____

Reason Selling: _____

Mortgage Balance: $ _____ Current (circle one)   Yes   No

Mortgage Payment: $ _____ Current (circle one)   Yes   No

Taxes: $ _____ Current (circle one)   Yes   No

Repair Items	Yes	No	Comments	Est. Repair Cost
Roof				
Carpeting				
Interior Paint				
Exterior Paint				
Furnace				
Central Air				
Kitchen				
Bathrooms				
Electric, upgrading required				
Replace windows				
Garage				
Basement				
Foundation/cracked or damaged				
Landscaping				
Miscellaneous (always include)				
Junky neighbors				

Additional Comments: _____
_____
_____

PROPERTY INSPECTION SHEET

Property Address: _____ Area (circle one) Good Fair Bad

Owner Name: _____ Phone: _____

Vacant: (circle one)   Yes   No

Construction: (circle one)   Brick   Frame   Other

No. of Bedrooms: _____ No. of Bathrooms: _____

Asking Price: $ _____

After Repair Value

(ARV): $ _____

Est. Repair Amt. $ _____

Maximum Offer $ _____

Reason Selling: _____

Mortgage Balance: $ _____ Current (circle one)   Yes   No

Mortgage Payment: $ _____ Current (circle one)   Yes   No

Taxes: $ _____ Current (circle one)   Yes   No

Repair Items	Yes	No	Comments	Est. Repair Cost
Roof				
Carpeting				
Interior Paint				
Exterior Paint				
Furnace				
Central Air				
Kitchen				
Bathrooms				
Electric, upgrading required				
Replace windows				
Garage				
Basement				
Foundation/cracked or damaged				
Landscaping				
Miscellaneous (always include)				
Junky neighbors				

Additional Comments: _____

_____

_____

COST ESTIMATE FOR REPAIRS AND SERVICES

Appraisals

Single Family Houses $275 for an As-Is Appraisal
$350 for a Subject to
$400

Inspections

Termite Inspection	$40
Building Inspection	$350
Survey	$195

Repairs

Item	Description	Est. Cost
Bathrooms	To renovate an entire bathroom	$1500–1700
Electric	To replace a service panel	$750–850
	To replace electric in entire single-family house	$4000–5000
	Electrician's approximate rate	$65/hr
Heating and Cooling	Furnace tune up	$55
	Air conditioner tune up	$59
	Gas forced air furnace, depending on how much new duct work is required	$1650
	New hot water boiler, depending on how much new piping is needed	$2300
	New air conditioner, depending on size of the unit	$1700
Kitchen	To replace kitchen with new cabinets, depending on the amount of cabinet space	$2500–3000

Item	Description	Est. Cost
Painting	Average painting job on a three-bedroom house, if there is a lot of drywall work and patching required increase your estimate accordingly. Any doubts, get a contractor's opinion.	$1300–1500
Plumbing	New hot water tank	$350
	Snake out drain	$100
	Plumber's average rate	$45/hr
Windows	Replacement windows (should include covering the outside of the window)	$250
Trash Removal	Dumpster rental	$350
	If house is totally trashed	$1750
Roofing	To replace the average roof on a three-bedroom house	$3200
Miscellaneous	Estimate costs for mistakes. This should make up for everything that you missed.	25% of the total renovation

REMEMBER:

When in doubt, always estimate high and get a contractor's opinion.

AGREEMENT OF SALE AND PURCHASE

Seller and Buyer, intending to be legally bound, agree as follows:

1. Parties, _____ (Buyer) and _____ (Seller) which terms may be singular or plural and will include the heir, successors, personal representatives and assigns of Seller and Buyer, hereby agree that Seller will sell and Buyer will buy the following property, upon the following terms and conditions:

2. Sale. Seller will grant and convey to Buyer by deed of <u>Special</u> warranty fee simple title to the land described in subparagraph A of this paragraph with the appurtenances and the buildings and improvements on the land (collectively the "Real Estate"). Title to the Real Estate will be good and marketable and will be free and clear of all encumbrances except as provided in paragraph 14. Title to the Real Estate will be insurable by any licensed title insurance company at regular rates.

   a) The land is located in_____County, Pennsylvania, and is described as follows:

   b) The sale and purchase will include the transfer to Buyer of the following items, free and clear of all encumbrances: (1) all plumbing, heating, cooling and electrical fixtures and systems, including chandeliers; (2) all built-ins (cabinets, cooking units and dishwasher); (3) fixtures; (4) all trees, screens, shades, venetian blinds, drapery rods and brackets, TV antenna and wall-to-wall carpeting. The following additional items are included in the sale: _____

   c) The Real Estate and the items in subparagraph B are called "Property" in this Agreement.

3. Purchase. Buyer will purchase the Property and pay to Seller the sum of $_____ payable as follows:

   a) Earnest Money Deposit in the amount of $_____, will be held in escrow by _____ until settlement.

   b) The balance by wire transfer, cashier check or certified at the time of delivery of deed.

4. Settlement. Settlement will be held in _____ County, Pennsylvania. Settlement will be held on _____, 20____. If settlement is not completed by this date either party will then have the right to declare time to be of the essence by giving notice to the other party. The notice will state that time is of the essence and will fix the time, date and place of settlement. The date fixed may not be earlier than 15 days or later than 30 days following the effective date of giving such notice.

5. Pre-Settlement Inspection. Buyer will be permitted, on reasonable notice and at a reasonable time prior to settlement, to inspect the Property which includes the items included in the sale in paragraph 2B.

6. Proration Items. Unless otherwise provided for in paragraph 20: (A) real estate transfer taxes will be shared equally between Seller and Buyer; (B) current water and sewer charges, municipal garbage and rubbish removal charges, rents, interest and real estate taxes will be prorated as of date of settlement; and (C) real estate taxes will be prorated on a calendar year basis for the calendar year of settlement based upon real estate taxes levied or estimated to be levied in that year by each taxing body without regard to the date of the levy or the fiscal year of the taxing body. Unless this Property is located in the City of Pittsburgh, real estate taxes levied by the local School District will be prorated on a fiscal year from July 1 through June 30.

7. Seller's Expense. Seller will pay the cost of deed preparation, title clearance and reasonable charges for settlement services and disbursements made on behalf of Seller.

8. Possession. Possession of the Property will be delivered to Buyer on date of settlement or as otherwise provided in paragraph 20. (If possession of the Property is to be delivered to Buyer prior to settlement or if Seller is to remain in possession of the Property after settlement, Seller and Buyer should execute a lease. If any part of the Property is occupied by a tenant, identify each lease in paragraph 20 and provide for assignment of each lease to Buyer.)

9. Risk of Loss: Insurance. Risk of loss of the Property will remain upon Seller until settlement. (Seller should have adequate fire and casualty insurance with extended coverage on the Property until settlement. Buyer may have an insurable interest in the Property

upon the signing of this Agreement. To protect Buyer's own interest, Buyer should have adequate fire and casualty insurance with extended coverage on the Property to protect Buyer's interest.)

10. Maintenance of the Property; Buyer's Option. Seller will maintain and make all repairs needed to keep the Property in as good condition as it is now, except for ordinary wear and tear. Seller will deliver the Property to Buyer broom clean, free of debris, with the lawn and shrubbery in trim. If a material change occurs in the physical condition of the Property before Buyer takes possession, Buyer will have the option to: (A) terminate this Agreement and upon termination all hand money will be returned immediately to Buyer after which the parties will be relieved of all obligations in this Agreement; or (B) proceed with this Agreement and pay the balance of the purchase price, and Seller will assign to Buyer any insurance proceeds to which Seller may be entitled as a result of the change in condition. To exercise this option Buyer will give notice to Seller before settlement. If Buyer fails to give the notice, Buyer will be conclusively deemed to have chosen option (B).

11. Eminent Domain; Buyer's Option. If any part of the Property is taken by eminent domain before settlement, Seller will notify Buyer of the taking within 5 days, but not later than the settlement. Buyer will have the option to (A) terminate this Agreement and upon termination all hand money will be returned immediately to Buyer after which the parties will be relieved of all obligations in this Agreement; or (B) proceed with this Agreement and pay the balance of the purchase price, and Seller will assign to Buyer the award, if any, to which Seller may be entitled. To exercise this option Buyer will give notice to Seller before settlement. If Buyer fails to give the notice, Buyer will be conclusively deemed to have chosen option (B).

12. Municipal Improvements. Seller will pay any municipal claim against the Property if the ordinance or resolution authorizing the work or improvement is adopted prior to the date of this Agreement. Buyer will pay any municipal claim against the Property if the ordinance or resolution authorizing the work or improvement is adopted on or after the date of this Agreement.

13. Default

   A) By Buyer. If Buyer defaults Seller may elect to: (1) retain the hand money as liquidated damages as the parties agree that the hand money is a reasonable settlement of Seller's damages and is not a penalty; if Seller chooses this remedy, upon notice to Buyer, this Agreement will be terminated and the parties released of further liability; or (2) apply the hand money toward Seller's damages which may include, but are not limited to, loss of bargain, consequential damages and attorney's fees prior to default. If Buyer defaults, all hand money will be divided equally between Seller and Broker, but in no event will the sum paid to Broker be in excess of the commission due Broker if no default occurred.

B) By Seller. If Seller defaults Buyer may elect to: (1) rescind this Agreement and waive any claim for loss of bargain; and if Buyer chooses this remedy, Seller will cause to be paid to Buyer the hand money and the direct costs which Buyer incurred in preparation for settlement, including, without limitation, title examination fees, mortgage loan fees and expenses, survey costs, inspection costs and attorney's fees prior to Seller's default; when Seller has made such payments in full to Buyer this Agreement will terminate; or (2) file an action for specific performance including consequential damages; or (3) file an action at law for damages for loss of bargain, Buyer's direct costs in preparation for settlement as set forth in subparagraph (1) of this paragraph B and consequential damages. Buyer may bring and continue either an action for specific performance or an action at law or both until final judgment.

14. Under and Subject. Buyer will take title to the Property subject to the following so long as they do not adversely affect the present use of the Property or at any time require removal or alteration of existing improvements: (A) building and use restrictions of record; (B) vehicular or pedestrian easements of record affecting the Property and being along the front, rear or side lot lines; (C) water, sewer, gas, electric, cable television, and telephone lines or easements therefor of record or as presently installed; (D) prior grants, reservations or leases of coal, oil, gas or other minerals as shown by instruments of record; and (E) easements apparent upon inspection of the Property.

15. Real Estate Broker. NONE

16. Broker's Commission. NONE

17. Notices Relating to Broker. NONE

18. Zoning and other Ordinances. Seller warrants that: The Property has the following Zoning Classification_____; the present use is _____ in compliance with that zoning classification; and there exists no notice of any uncorrected violations of housing, building, safety or fire ordinances. (For settlement, obtain statements as to compliance and non-violation, if required.)

19. Inspection of Property. Buyer acknowledges that Buyer inspected the Property before signing this Agreement. Buyer is relying only on the inspection of the Property made by Buyer and is not relying on any oral statement concerning the physical condition of the Property given to Buyer by Seller or Broker except for written statements contained in this Agreement.

20. Additional Provisions.

21. Sewage Facility Notice. _____Check here if there is no currently existing community sewage system serving the property. If no currently existing community sewage system is available to the Property, the Pennsylvania Sewage Facilities Act of January 24, 1966, No. 537 P.L. 1535, as amended, requires the following statement:

    Buyer is hereby advised that there is no currently existing community sewage system available to the Property and that a permit for an individual sewage system will have to be obtained from the appropriate local agency pursuant to the Pennsylvania Sewage Facilities Act. Buyer should contact the appropriate local agency which administers the Pennsylvania Sewage Facilities Act before signing this Agreement to determine the procedure and requirements for obtaining a permit for an individual sewage system if one has not already been obtained.

22. Coal Notice. Notice this document may not sell, convey, transfer, include or insure the title to the coal and right to support underneath the surface land described or referred to herein, and the owner or owners of such coal may have the complete legal right to remove all of such coal and in that connection, damage may result to the surface of the land and any house, building or other structure on or in such land. The inclusion of this notice does not enlarge, restrict or modify any legal rights or estates otherwise created, transferred,

excepted or reserved by this instrument. (This notice is set forth in the manner provided in Section 1 of the Act of July 17, 1957, P.L. 984, as amended, and is not intended as notice of unrecorded instruments, if any.) Unless this notice is stricken, the deed for the Property will contain this notice and will also contain, and Buyer will sign, the notice specified in the Bituminous Mine Subsidence and Land Conservation Act of 1966.

23. Waiver of Tender. Formal tender of a deed for the Property by Seller to Buyer is waived by Buyer. Formal tender of the balance of the purchase price by Buyer to Seller is waived by Seller.

24. Notice to Parties. Any notice given by Seller to Buyer or by Buyer to Seller will be in writing. Any notices will be delivered either in the manner provided by law for the service of process in equity or by certified or registered mail to the receiving party at the address for the receiving party which appears on the first page of this Agreement. Any mailed notice will be deemed delivered to the receiving party on the second business day after mailing occurs.

25. Covenant not to Record. Buyer will not record this Agreement and any recording of this Agreement by Buyer will constitute a default by Buyer under this Agreement.

26. Binding Effect. Seller and Buyer intend to be legally bound by this Agreement. All of its terms and conditions will extend to and be binding upon the parties to this Agreement and upon their respective heirs, executors, administrators, personal representatives, successors and assigns.

27. Interpretation. This Agreement constitutes the entire contract between the parties and there are no other understandings, oral or written, relating to the sale and purchase of the Property. This Agreement may not be changed, modified, or amended, in whole or in part, except in another writing, signed by all parties. Wherever used in this Agreement, the singular will include the plural, the plural the singular, and the use of any gender will be applicable to all genders. Paragraph headings and italicized clauses are inserted for convenience only and will not form part of the text of this Agreement.

THIS IS A LEGALLY BINDING CONTRACT. IF NOT FULLY
UNDERSTOOD, CONSULT YOUR ATTORNEY PRIOR TO SIGNING.

Signed by Buyer this_____ day of_____, 20____.

_____

_____
_____(Seal)
        witness   buyer

_____

_____
_____(Seal)
        witness   buyer

Signed by Seller this_____ day of_____, 20____.

_____

_____
_____(Seal)
        witness   seller

_____

_____
_____(Seal)
        witness   seller

CONTRACTOR'S BID

Patterson General Contractors
1347 Lakewood Street
Pittsburgh, PA 15220

Date: 7-17-2003
Estimate #:   34

Name/Address

REAL ESTATE EXPRESS

Project

Description	Qty	Rate	Total
7x12 kitchen floor/sub floor		445.00	445.00
24 inch vanity and mirror/faucet		295.00	295.00
Toilet seat		15.00	15.00
24 inch light	1	95.00	95.00
Tub replace tub vinyl caulk strip		0.00	
1 gfi in bath	1	55.00	55.00
3 outlets in small bedroom	3	45.00	135.00
Paint and primer		1,350.00	1,350.00
3 interior doors six panel	3	135.00	405.00
Ceiling fan in master	1	165.00	165.00
New fixtures	3	80.00	240.00
Oak light fixture in kitchen area	1	195.00	195.00
Repair concrete steps in front area (unknown cost, must remove carpet to assess damage)			
carpet 115 yards		1,265.00	1,265.00

TOTAL			$ 4,660.00

PROOF OF INSURANCE

Certificate of Liability Insurance

Producer:
Alan E. Jones
240 Steubenville Pike
McKees Rocks, PA 15136
(412)555-1111

Insured:
Bernard Smith
555 Danvers Ave.
Pittsburgh, PA 15205

This certificate is issued as a matter of information only and confers no rights upon the certificate holder. This certificate does not amend, extend or alter the coverage afforded by the policies below.

INSURERS AFFORDING COVERAGE
Insurer A: Mutual Benefit Insurance Co.
Insurer B:
Insurer C:
Insurer D:
Insurer E:

COVERAGES

THE POLICIES OF INSURANCE LISTED BELOW HAVE BEEN ISSUED TO THE INSURED NAMED ABOVE FOR THE POLICY PERIOD INDICATED, NOTWITHSTANDING ANY REQUIREMENT, TERM OR CONDITION OF ANY CONTRACT OR OTHER DOCUMENT WITH RESPECT TO WHICH THIS CERTIFICATE MAY BE ISSUED OR MAY PERTAIN. THE INSURANCE AFFORDED BY THE POLICIES DESCRIBED HEREIN IS SUBJECT TO ALL THE TERMS, EXCLUSIONS AND CONDITIONS OF SUCH POLICIES. AGGREGATE LIMITS SHOWN MAY HAVE BEEN REDUCED BY PAID CLAIMS.

NSR LTR	TYPE OF INSURANCE	POLICY NUMBER	POLICY EFFECTIVE DATE (MM/DD/YY)	POLICY EXPIRATION DATE (MM/DD/YY)	LIMITS	
A	GENERAL LIABILITY X Commercial General Liability __ __ claims made ___ occur	AC00911425	03/19/01	03/19/02	Each occurrence	1,000,000
					Fire damage (any one fire)	100,000
					Med Exp (Any one person)	10,000
					Personal and Adv injury	1,000,000
	General Aggregate Limit applies per:				General Aggregate	2,000,000
	___ policy project loc				Products-comp/op agg	1,000,000
	AUTOMOTIVE LIABILITY				Combined Single Limit (Ea accident)	
	Any Auto				Bodily Injury	
	All Owned Autos				(Per Person)	
	Scheduled Autos				Bodily Injury	
	Hired Autos				(Per Accident)	
	Non-Owned Autos				Property Damage (Per Accident)	
	GARAGE LIABILITY				Auto only - Ea accident	
	Any Auto				Other than Ea acc	
					Auto only: agg	
	EXCESS LIABILITY				Each occurrence	
	Occur Claims made				Aggregate	
	Deductible					
	Retention					

WORKERS' COMPENSATION AND EMPLOYERS' LIABILITY				WC STATUTORY LIMITS	OTHER
				EL Ea Accident	100,000
A	WC00911425	03/19/01	03/19/02	EL disease-ea employee	100,000
				EL disease-policy limit	500,000
OTHER					

DESCRIPTION OF OPERATIONS/LOCATIONS/VEHICLES/EXCLUSIONS ADDED BY ENDORSEMENT/SPECIAL PROVISIONS

PLUMBING

CERTIFICATE HOLDER	ADDITIONAL INSURED; INSURER LETTER:	CANCELLATION
HOUSES UNLIMITED 3049 CHARTIERS AVE. PITTSBURGH, PA 15204		Should any of the above described policies be canceled before the expiration date thereof, the issuing insurer will endeavor to Mail 10 days written notice to the certificate holder named to the left, but failure to do so shall impose no obligation or liability of any kind upon the insurer, its agents or representatives.

Authorized Representative

FORM W-9

Form W-9	Request for Taxpayer Identification Number and Certification

(Rev. Dec 1996)
Dept of the Treasury
Internal Revenue Service

Name (if a joint account or you changed your name, see Specific Instructions on page 2)

Business Name, if different from above (See Specific Instructions on page 2)

Check appropriate box: | | Individual/sole proprietor | | Corporation | | Partnership | | Other

Address (number, street, and apt. or suite no.)   Requestor's name and address (optional)

City, state, and ZIP code

PART I Taxpayer Identification Number (TIN)   List account number(s) here (optional)

Enter your TIN in the appropriate box. For individuals, this is your social security number (SSN). However, if you are a resident alien OR a sole proprietor, see the instructions on page 2. For other entities, it is your employer identification number (EIN). If you do not have a number, see How To Get a TIN on page 2.

Social security number

OR

PART II For Payees Exempt From Backup Withholding (See the instructions on Page 2)

Note: If the account is in more than one name, see the chart on page 2 for guidelines on whose number to enter.

Employer identification number

Part III Certification

Under penalties of perjury, I certify that:

1. The number shown on this form is my correct taxpayer identification number (or I am waiting for a number to be issued to me), and
2. I am not subject to backup withholding because: (a) I am exempt from backup withholding, or (b) I have not been notified by the Internal Revenue Service (IRS) that I am subject to backup withholding as a result of a failure to report all interest or dividends, or (c) the IRS has notified me that I am no longer subject to backup withholding.

Certification Instructions. You must cross out Item 2 above if you have been notified by the IRS that you are currently subject to backup withholding because you have failed to report all interest and dividends on your tax return. For real estate transactions, item 2 does not apply. For mortgage interest paid, acquisition or abandonment of secured property, cancellation of debt, contributions to an individual retirement arrangement (IRA), and generally payments other than interest and dividends, you are not required to sign the Certification, but you must provide your correct TIN. (See the Instructions on Page 2)

Sign
Here   Signature ➤   Date ➤

Purpose of Form. - A person who is required to file an information return with the IRS must get your correct taxpayer identification number (TIN) to report, for example, income paid to you, real estate transactions, mortgage interest you paid, acquisition or abandonment of secured property, cancellation of debt, or contributions you made to an IRA.

Use Form W-9 to give your correct TIN to the person requesting it (the requester) and, when applicable, to:

1) Certify the TIN you are giving is correct (or you are waiting for a number to be issued).
2) Certify you are not subject to backup withholding, or
3) Claim exemption from backup withholding if you are an exempt payee.

Note: If a requester gives you a form other than a W-9 to request your TIN, you must use the requester's form if it is substantially similar to this Form W-9.

What is Backup Withholding? - Persons making certain payments to you must withhold and pay to the IRS 31% of such payments under certain conditions. This is called "backup withholding."

Payments that may be subject to backup withholding include interest, dividends, broker and barter exchange transactions, rents, royalties, nonemployee pay, and certain payments from fishing boat operators. Real estate transactions are not subject to backup withholding.

If you give the requester your correct TIN, make the proper certifications, and report all your taxable interest and dividends on your tax return, payments you receive will not be subject to backup withholding. Payments you receive will be subject to backup withholding if:

1) You do not furnish your TIN to the requester, or

2) The IRS tells the requester that you furnished an incorrect TIN, or

3) The IRS tells you that you are subject to backup withholding because you did not report all your interest and dividends on your tax return (for reportable interest and dividends only), or

4) You do not certify to the requester that you are not subject to backup withholding under 3 above (for reportable interest and dividend accounts opened after 1983 only), or

5) You do not certify your TIN when required. See the Part III Instructions on page 2 for details.

Certain payees and payments are exempt from backup withholding. See the Part II Instructions and the separate Instructions for the Requester of Form W-9.

Penalties
Failure to Furnish TIN - If you fail to furnish your correct TIN to a requester, you are subject to a penalty of $50 for each such failure unless your failure is due to reasonable cause and not to willful neglect.

Civil Penalty for False Information With Respect to Withholding - If you make a false statement with no reasonable basis that results in no backup withholding, you are subject to a $500 penalty.

Criminal Penalty for Falsifying Information - Willfully falsifying certifications or affirmations may subject you to criminal penalties including fines and/or imprisonment.

Misuse of TINs - If the requester discloses or uses TINs in violation of Federal law, the requester may be subject to civil and criminal penalties.

SELLER DISCLOSURE STATEMENT

This Form May Only Be Certified To By The Seller

Seller Information

Seller(s) Name(s): _____

Property Address (Mailing Address and Municipality of Property) (Hereinafter referred to as the "Property"): _____

Approximate Age of Property:_____   Years Seller has owned Property:

NOTICE TO PARTIES

A Seller must disclose to a Buyer all known material defects about the Property being sold that are not readily observable. This Disclosure Statement is designed to assist the Seller in complying with disclosure requirements and to assist the Buyer in evaluating the Property being considered.

This statement discloses the Seller's knowledge of the condition of the Property as of the date signed by the Seller and is not a substitute for any inspections or warranties that the Buyer may wish to obtain. This statement is not a warranty of any kind by the Seller or a warranty or representation by any listing real estate broker, any selling real estate broker or their agents. The Buyer is encouraged to address concerns about the conditions of the Property that may not be included in this statement. This statement does not relieve the Seller of the obligation to disclose a material defect that may not be addressed on this form.

If an item of information is unknown or not available to Seller and Seller has made an effort to ascertain it, Seller may make a disclosure based on the best information available provided it is identified as a disclosure based on an incomplete factual basis.

A material defect is a problem with the Property or any portion of it that would have a significant adverse impact on the value of the residential real Property or that INVOLVES AN UNREASONABLE RISK TO PEOPLE ON THE LAND.

1. SELLER'S EXPERTISE

The Seller does not possess expertise in contracting, engineering, architecture or other areas related to the construction and conditions of the Property and its improvements, except as follows:

_____

2. OCCUPANCY

(a) Do you, the Seller, currently occupy this Property? Yes_____ No_____ If "No", when did you last occupy the Property? _____(Year)

(b) Is the Property zoned for single family residential use? Yes_____
No_____ Unknown_____
(c) Will a Certificate of Occupancy be required by the Municipality and/or
government unit? Yes_____ No_____

3. ROOF

(a) Date roof was installed: _____
Documented: Yes_____ No_____ Unknown_____
(b) Has the roof been replaced, repaired, or overlaid during your
ownership? Yes_____ No_____
(c) Has the roof ever leaked during your ownership? Yes_____ No_____
(d) Do you know of any problems with the roof, gutters or downspouts?
Yes_____ No_____
Explain any "Yes" answers that you give in this section:

_____

_____

4. BASEMENTS, GARAGES AND CRAWL SPACES (COMPLETE ONLY IF APPLICABLE):

(a) Does the Property have a sump pump or grinder pump? Yes_____
No_____ Unknown_____
(b) Are you aware of any water leakage, accumulation or dampness within
the basement, garage or crawl space?   Yes_____ No_____
If "Yes", describe in detail: _____
(c) Do you know of any repairs or other attempts to control any water or
dampness problem in the basement, garage or crawl space? Yes_____
No_____
If "Yes", describe the location, extent, date and name of the person who did
the repair or control effort:_____

5. TERMITES/WOOD DESTROYING INSECTS, DRY ROT, PESTS

(a) Are you aware of any termites/wood destroying insects, dry rot or pests
affecting the Property? Yes_____ No_____
(b) Are you aware of any damage to the Property caused by termites/wood
destroying insects, dry rot or pests? Yes_____ No_____
(c) Is your Property currently under contract by a licensed pest control
company? Yes_____ No_____
(d) Are you aware of any termite/pest control reports or treatments to the
Property? Yes_____ No_____
Explain any "Yes" answers that you give in this section:

_____

_____

6.   STRUCTURAL ITEMS

(a) Are you aware of any past or present water leakage in the house or other structure? Yes_____ No_____
(b) Are you aware of any past or present movement, shifting, deterioration or other problem with walls, foundations or other structural components? Yes_____ No_____
(c) Are you aware of any past or present problems with driveways, walkways, patios or retaining walls on the Property? Yes_____ No_____
(d) Have there been any repairs or other attempts to remedy or control the cause or effect of any defects or conditions described above? Yes_____ No_____ Unknown_____
(e) Are you aware of any problem with the use or operation of the windows? Yes_____ No_____
(f) Has there ever been fire damage to the property? Yes_____ No_____ Unknown_____
Explain any "Yes" answers that you give in this section. When explaining efforts to control or repair, please describe the location and extent of the problem and the date and person by whom the work was done, if known:

_____

_____

7.   ADDITIONS/REMODELING

(a) Have you made any additions, structural changes or other alterations to the Property? Yes_____ No_____
If "Yes", please describe: _____

_____
(b) Did you obtain all necessary permits and approvals and was all work in compliance with building codes? Yes_____ No_____ Unknown_____
(c) Did any former owners of the Property make any additions, structural changes or other alterations to the Property? Yes_____ No_____ Unknown_____
If "Yes", to the best of your knowledge, did they obtain all necessary permits and approvals, and was all work in compliance with building codes? Yes_____ No_____ Unknown _____

8.   WATER AND SEWAGE

(a) What is the source of your drinking water? public_____ community system_____ well on Property_____ other_____
If "other", please explain: _____
(b) If your drinking water source is not public: When was your water last tested?_____ What was the result of the test?_____
Is the pumping system in working order? Yes_____ No_____ If "No", please explain: _____

(c) Do you have a water softener, filter or other purification system?
Yes_____ No_____ If "Yes", is the system leased_____ owned_____
(d) What is the type of sewage system? Public sewer_____ individual on-lot
sewage system_____ individual on-lot sewage disposal system in proximity
to well_____ community sewage disposal system_____ ten acre permit
exemption_____ holding tank_____ cesspool_____ septic tank_____ sand
mound_____ none_____ none available/permit limitations in effect_____
other_____ If "Other",
please explain: _____

9. PLUMBING SYSTEM

(a) Type of plumbing: copper_____ galvanized_____ lead_____ PVC_____
mixed_____ unknown_____ other_____
If "Other", please explain:
(b) Are you aware of any problems with any of your plumbing fixtures
(including, but not limited to, kitchen, laundry or bathroom fixtures, wet bars,
hot water heater, etc.)? Yes_____ No_____
If "Yes", please explain: _____

10. HEATING AND AIR CONDITIONING

(a) Type of air conditioning: central electric_____ central gas_____
wall_____ none_____ Number of window units included in sale_____
Location: _____
(b) List of any areas of the house that are not air conditioned: _____
_____
(c) Type of heating: electric____ fuel oil____ natural gas____ other_____
If "Other", please explain: _____
(d) List of any areas of the house that are not heated: _____
_____
(e) Type of water heating: electric_____ gas_____ solar_____ other_____ If
"other", please explain:_____
(f) If there are fireplaces in the Property, are they operational? Yes_____
No_____
(g) Are you aware of any underground fuel tanks on the Property?
Yes_____ No_____
If "Yes", please describe: _____
_____
(h) Are you aware of any problems with any item in this section? Yes_____
No_____
If "Yes", please explain:
_____

11. ELECTRICAL SYSTEM

Are you aware of any problems or repairs needed in the electrical system?
Yes_____ No_____
If "Yes", please explain: _____
_____

12. OTHER EQUIPMENT AND APPLIANCES INCLUDED IN SALE (COMPLETE WHERE APPLICABLE):

(a) _____ Electrical garage door opener/Number of transmitters_____ Are
they in working order? Yes__ No__
(b) _____ Smoke detectors/How many? _____ Location: _____
_____
(c) _____ Security alarm system: Owned_____ Leased_____ Lease
information: _____
(d) _____ Lawn sprinkler   Number_____ Automatic timer_____ In working
order? Yes_____ No_____
(e) _____ Swimming pool_____ Pool heater_____Automatic timer_____ In
working order? Yes____ No_____
(f) _____ Refrigerator_____ Range_____ Microwave Oven_____
Dishwasher_____ Trash Compactor _____Garbage disposal
(g) _____ Washer_____ Dryer
(h) _____ Intercom
(i) _____ Ceiling fans_____ Number Location: _____
(j) Other: _____
Are any items in this section in need of repair or replacement? Yes_____
No_____ Unknown_____
If "Yes", please explain: _____

13. LAND (SOILS, DRAINAGE AND BOUNDARIES):

(a) Are you aware of any fill or expansive soil on the Property? Yes_____
No_____
(b) Are you aware of any sliding, settling, earth movement, upheaval,
subsidence or earth stability problems that have occurred on or that affect
the Property? Yes_____ No_____

NOTE TO THE BUYER: THE PROPERTY MAY BE SUBJECT TO MINE SUBSIDENCE DAMAGE. MAPS OF THE COUNTIES AND MINES WHERE MINE SUBSIDENCE DAMAGE MAY OCCUR AND MINE SUBSIDENCE INSURANCE ARE AVAILABLE THROUGH: DEPARTMENT OF ENVIRONMENTAL PROTECTION, MINE SUBSIDENCE INSURANCE FUND, 3913 WASHINGTON ROAD, MCMURRAY, PA 15317 (412) 941-7100.

(c) Are you aware of any existing or proposed mining, strip mining or any
other excavations that might affect this Property? Yes_____ No_____

(d) To your knowledge, is this Property, or part of it, located in a flood zone or wetlands area? Yes____ No____

(e) Do you know of any past or present drainage or flooding problems affecting the Property or adjacent properties?   Yes_____ No_____

(f) Do you know of any encroachments, boundary line disputes, rights of way or easements? Yes____ No____

NOTE TO BUYER: Most properties have easements running across them for utility services and other reasons. In many cases, the easements do not restrict the ordinary use of the Property, and the Seller may not be readily aware of them. Buyers may wish to determine the existence of easements and restrictions by examining the Property and ordering an abstract of title or searching the records in the Office of the Recorder of Deeds for the County before entering into an agreement of sale.

(g) Are you aware of any shared or common areas (for example, driveways, bridges, docks, walls, etc.) or maintenance agreements? Yes_____ No_____

Explain any "Yes" answers that you give in this section: _____

_____

(h) Do you have an existing survey of the Property? Yes_____ No_____ If "Yes", has the survey been made available to the Listing Real Estate Broker? Yes_____ No_____

(i) Does the Property abut a public road? Yes_____ No_____ If not, is there a recorded right-of-way and maintenance agreement to a public road? Yes_____ No_____

14. HAZARDOUS SUBSTANCES

(a) Are you aware of any underground tanks or hazardous substances present on the Property (structure or soil), including, but not limited to, asbestos, polychlorinated biphenyls (PCBs), radon, lead paint, urea-formaldehyde foam insulation (UFFI), etc.? Yes_____ No_____

(b) To your knowledge, has the Property been tested for any hazardous substances? Yes_____ No_____

(c) Do you know of any other environmental concerns that might impact upon the Property? Yes____ No_____

Explain any "Yes" answers that you give in this section:

(d) Lead-Based Paint Hazard Reduction Act.

(a) Was this house constructed prior to 1978? Yes_____ No_____ Unknown_____

(b) Is Seller aware of the presence of any lead-based paint hazards in the Property?   Yes_____ *No_____ *Is the test report available?

(c) NOTE: If the house was built prior to 1978, Seller and Seller's Agent must disclose any lead-based paint information which they have, furnish a Lead Hazard Information Pamphlet to any prospective Buyer and advise Buyer of his rights under the Act.

(d) Do you have any report or records relating to any tests that have been performed on your property regarding hazardous substances? Yes_____ No_____

15. CONDOMINIUMS AND OTHER HOMEOWNERS ASSOCIATIONS (COMPLETE ONLY IF APPLICABLE)

(a) Type: Condominium_____ Cooperative_____ Homeowners Association_____ Other_____
If "Other", please explain: _____
_____

Notice regarding Condominiums, Cooperatives and Homeowners Associations: According to Section 3407 of the Uniform Condominium Act (68 Pa.C.S. §3407) (Relating to resales of Units) and 68 Pa.C.S. §4409 (Relating to resales of cooperative interests) and Section 5407 of the Uniform Planned Community Act (68 Pa.C.S.A. 5407), a Buyer of a resale Unit must receive a Certificate of Resale issued by the Association. The Buyer will have the option of canceling the Agreement with return of all deposit moneys until the Certificate has been provided to the Buyer and for five days thereafter or until conveyance, whichever occurs first. The Seller must be sure the Buyer receives a Resale Certificate.
(b) Do you know of any defect, damage or problem with any common elements or common areas which could affect their value or desirability? Yes_____ No_____ Unknown_____
(c) Do you know of any condition or claim which may result in an increase in assessments or fees? Yes_____ No _____ Unknown_____
If your answer to (b) or (c) is "Yes", explain in detail: _____
_____

16. MISCELLANEOUS

(a) Are you aware of any existing or threatened legal action affecting the Property? Yes_____ No_____
(b) Do you know of any violations of Federal, State or local laws or regulations relating to this Property?   Yes_____ No_____
(c) Are you aware of any public improvement, condominium or homeowner association assessments against the Property that remain unpaid or of any violations of zoning, housing, building, safety or fire ordinances that remain uncorrected? Yes_____ No_____
(d) Are you aware of any judgment, encumbrance, lien (for example, comaker or equity loan) or other debt against this property that cannot be satisfied by the proceeds of this sale? Yes____ No_____
(e) Are you aware of any reason, including a defect in title, that would prevent you from giving a warranty deed or conveying title to the Property? Yes_____ No_____
(f) Are you aware of any material defects to the Property, dwelling or fixtures which are not disclosed elsewhere on this form?   Yes_____ No_____

A material defect is a problem with the Property or any portion of it that would have significant adverse impact on the value of the residential real Property or that INVOLVES AN UNREASONABLE RISK TO PEOPLE ON THE LAND.
Explain any "Yes" answers that you give in this section: _____
_____

(g) Is there any additional information that you feel you should disclose to a prospective Buyer because it may materially and substantially affect the value or desirability of the Property, e.g., zoning violation, set back violations, zoning changes, road changes, pending municipal improvements, pending tax assessment appeals, etc.? Yes_____ No_____ Unknown_____
If your answers in this section are "Yes", explain in detail: _____
_____

The undersigned Seller represents that the information set forth in this Disclosure Statement is accurate and complete to the best of the Seller's knowledge. The Seller hereby authorizes any agent for the Seller to provide this information to prospective Buyers of the Property and to other real estate agents. *The Seller alone is responsible for the accuracy of the information contained in this statement.* The Seller shall cause the Buyer to be notified in writing of any information supplied on this form which is rendered inaccurate by a change in the condition of the Property following the completion of this form.

West Penn Multi-List, Inc. has not participated, in any way, in the preparation of the answers in this statement.
Every Seller Signing Listing Contract must sign this statement.

SELLER _____   DATE _____

SELLER _____   DATE _____

EXECUTOR, ADMINISTRATOR, TRUSTEE, COURT APPOINTED GUARDIAN, RECORDED POWER OF ATTORNEY

The undersigned has never occupied the Property and lacks the personal knowledge necessary to complete this Disclosure Statement.

_____   DATE _____

_____   DATE _____
Please Indicate Capacity / Title of Person Signing Plus Include Documentation

CORPORATE LISTING

The undersigned has never occupied the Property. Any information contained in this Disclosure Statement was obtained from third party sources and Buyer should satisfy himself or herself as to the condition of the Property.

_____ DATE _____
Please Indicate Capacity / Title of Person Signing Plus Include Documentation

RECEIPT AND ACKNOWLEDGMENT BY BUYER

BUYER _____ DATE _____

BUYER _____ DATE _____

The undersigned Buyer acknowledges receipt of this Disclosure Statement. The Buyer acknowledges that this statement is not a warranty and that, unless stated otherwise in the sales contract, the Buyer is purchasing this Property in its present condition. It is the Buyer's responsibility to satisfy himself or herself as to the condition of the Property. The Buyer may request that the property be inspected, at the Buyer's expense by a full member in good standing of a national home inspection association in accordance with the ethical standards and code of conduct or practice of that association. Buyer may request the property be inspected and obtain a written Home Inspection Report which describes the condition of the property and discloses material defects. Buyer acknowledges and understands that an Agent of a Seller or Buyer is not liable for any material defect that was not disclosed to the Buyer or for any misrepresentation relating to a material defect unless the Agent had actual knowledge of the material defect. Buyer acknowledges their understanding of the right to request a home inspection. Therefore, Buyer hereby releases Agent of Seller or Buyer from any and all claims arising out of a failure to disclose a material defect with the exception of those material defects Agent had specific knowledge of. Attached hereto and made a part hereof is the Pennsylvania Home Inspection Compliance Statement as prepared by the Pennsylvania Home Inspection Compliance Statement to the Home Inspector of their choice so that this form can be attached to the Home Inspection Report.

HUD-1 SETTLEMENT SHEET

U.S. DEPARTMENT OF HOUSING AND URBAN DEVELOPMENT

B: TYPE OF LOAN   246/119

1. { } FHA   2. { } PMMA   3. { } CONV. UNINS.   6. File Number   7. Loan Number   8. Mtg. Ins. No.

4. { } VA   5. { } CONV. INS.   03-167010   -

C. NOTE: This form is furnished to give a statement of actual settlement costs. Amounts paid to and by the
settlement agent are shown. Items marked "p.o.c." were paid outside of closing; they are shown here for
informational purposes and not included in the totals.

D: NAME & ADDRESS OF BORROWER   E: NAME & ADDRESS OF SELLER   F: NAME & ADDRESS OF LENDER

John Smith	Patrick Beck and Carol Beck	Community Investment Group One Oxford Centre, Ste. 450 Pittsburgh, PA 15219
	TIN TIN	

G: PROPERTY LOCATION

114 2nd Street
Pittsburgh
PA 15219

H: SETTLEMENT AGENT
Hirshberg, Gustine & Straka, LLP
One Oxford Centre, Ste. 450
Pittsburgh, PA 15219 (412)391-9200
PLACE OF SETTLEMENT   Pittsburgh, PA
I: SETTLEMENT DATE   9/02/2003

J: SUMMARY OF BUYER'S TRANSACTIONS		K: SUMMARY OF SELLER'S TRANSACTIONS	
100 GROSS AMOUNT DUE FROM BORROWER		400 GROSS AMOUNT DUE TO SELLERS	
101 Contract Sales Price	$ 28,500.00	401 Contract sales price	$ 28,500.00
102 Personal property		402 Personal property	
103 Settlement charges to borrower (From line 1400)	$ 11,560.61	403	
104		404	
105		405	
Adjustments for Items Paid by Seller in Advance		Adjustments for Items Paid by Seller in Advance	
106 City/town tax 9/3/2003 to 12/31/2003	$ 32.34	406 City/town tax 9/3/2003 to 12/31/2003	$ 32.34
107 County taxes 9/3/20-03 to 12/31/2003	$ 34.36	407 County taxes 9/3/2003 to 12/31/2003	$ 34.36
108 School taxes 9/3/2003 to 12/31/2003	$ 254.58	408 School taxes 9/3/2003 to 12/31/2003	$ 254.58
109 Assessments		409 Assessments	
110		410	
111		411	
112		412	
120 Gross Amount Due from Borrower	$ 40,382.29	420 Gross Amount Due to Seller:	$ 28,821.68
200 AMOUNTS PAID BY OR IN BEHALF OF BORROWER:		500 REDUCTIONS IN AMOUNT DUE TO SELLER:	
201 Earnest or deposit money		501 Earnest or deposit money	
202 Principal amount of new loan	$ 36,000.00	502 Settlement charges to seller-line 1400	$ 321.58
203 Existing loans taken subject to		503 Existing loans taken subject to	
204		504 Payoff of first mortgage loan	
205		to:	
206 2ⁿᵈ note from Houses	$ 3,000.00	Express Mail/Courier charges	
207 3ʳᵈ note Community Investment	$ 492.49	507	
208		508	
209		509	
Adjustments for Items Unpaid by Seller		Adjustments for Items Unpaid by Seller	
210 City/local tax		510 City/local tax	
211 County taxes		511 County taxes	
212 School taxes		512 School taxes	
213 Assessments		513 Assessments	
214 Sewage credit		514 Sewage credit	
215		515 ESCROW TO:	
216		516	
217		517	
218		518	
219		519 **Seller Agrees to Pay Final Water Bill**	
220 Total Paid by/for Borrower:	$ 39,382.49	520 Total Reductions in Amount due Seller	$ 321.58
300 CASH AT SETTLEMENT TO/FROM BORROWER		600 CASH AT SETTLEMENT TO/FROM SELLER	
301 Gross amount due from borrower (line 120)	$ 40,382.49	601 Gross amount due to seller (line 420)	$ 28,821.68

| 302 Less amounts paid by/for borrower | $37,382.49 | 602 Less reductions in amount due seller | $ 321.58 |
| 303 CASH FROM BORROWER | $ 1,000.00 | 603 CASH TO SELLER | $ 28,500.10 |

SUBSTITUTE FORM 1099 SELLER STATEMENT

The information contained in blocks E, G, H and I and on line 401 (or, if line 401 is asterisked, lines 403 and 404) is important tax information and is being furnished to the Internal Revenue Service. If you are required to file a return, a negligence penalty or other sanctions will be imposed on you if this item is required to be reported and the IRS determines that it has not been reported.

You are required by law to provide   Hirshberg, Gustine & Straka, LLP
with your correct taxpayer identification number. If you do not do so, you may be subject to civil or criminal penalties imposed by law. Under penalties or perjury, I certify that the number shown on this statement is my correct taxpayer identification number.

Seller's signature _____   _____
                        Patrick Marino   Carol Marino

SELLER'S INSTRUCTIONS

If this real estate was your principal residence, file Form 2119, Sale or Exchange of Principal Residence, for any gain, with your income tax return; for other transactions, compete the applicable parts of Form 4797, Form 6252 and/or Schedule D, Form 1040.

L:	12:14 SETTLEMENT CHARGES		02-Sep-2003	Paid From Borrower's Funds at Settlement	Paid From Seller's Funds at Settlement
700	Broker's Commission based on price		$28,500.00		
	Commission rate				
	Division of Commission Below				
701					
702					
703	Commission paid at settlement				
704					
800	ITEMS PAYABLE IN CONNECTION WITH LOAN				
801	Loan origination fee	10.000%	Community Investment Group	$ 3,600.00	
802	Loan discount		Community Investment Group		
803	Appraisal fee	$ 350.00	Rock Appraisal	$ 350.00	
804	Credit report to	$ 20.00	Community Investment Services	$ 20.00	
805	ESCROW REPAIR	$ 1,000.00	Community Investment Group	$ 1,000.00	
806	Service Release PREN:		Yield Spread:		
807	Assignment Fee		Houses Unlimited	$ 3,000.00	
808	Doc. Prep to Lender:		Community Investment Group	$ 350.00	
809	Processing Fee		Community Investment Group	$ 200.00	
810	Flood Certification		Community Investment Group		
900	ITEMS REQUIRED BY LENDER TO BE PAID IN ADVANCE				
901	Interest from / to 9/03/2003	9/30/2003	8.225		$ 230.30
902	Mortgage insurance premium for	12 months to			
903	Hazard insurance premium	1 year			
904		TO:			
905					
1000	RESERVES DEPOSITED WITH LENDER				
1001	Hazard insurance		months at		
1002	Mortgage insurance		months at		
1003	City property taxes		months at		
1004	County property taxes		months at		
1005	School taxes		months at		
1006	Annual assessments		months at		
1007			TOTAL:		
1008	Aggregate Accounting Adjustment				
1100	TITLE CHARGES				
1101	Settlement or closing fee Hirshberg, Gustine & Straka, LLP			$ 100.00	
1102	Abstract of title search				
1103	Title examination				
1104	Title insurance binder				

1105	Document preparation	Hirshberg, Gustine & Straka, LLP	$ 275.00	
1106	Notary fees	Hirshberg, Gustine & Straka, LLP	$ 10.00	
1107	Atty fees TO:			
	(Includes above items No.:			
1108	Title insurance	Hirshberg, Gustine & Straka, LLP	BASIC	$ 463.50
	(Includes above items No.:		$463.50	
1109	Lender's coverage	$36,000.00		
1110	Owner's coverage	$28,500.00		
1111				
1112				

1200	GOVERNMENT RECORDING AND TRANSFER CHARGES			
1201	Recording fee: deed	$37.50 Mortgage $65.00	$ 102.50	
1202	City/county tax stamps	2.50%	$ 712.50	$ 0.00
1203	State tax/stamps	1.00%	$ 181.95	$ 103.05
1204	Additional recording fees			
1205	Additional recording fees			
1300	ADDITIONAL SETTLEMENT CHARGES			
1301	Survey to:	Bock & Clark	$ 195.00	
1302	Pest Inspection			
1303	Lien letters to:	Hirshberg, Gustine & Straka, LLP		$ 101.00
1304	Waste Management	Garbage		$ 22.95
1305	Central Tax Bureau of PA, Inc.	Sewage		$ 94.58
1306	Borough of McKees Rocks	Borough 2003	$ 880.06	
1307				
1400	Total Settlement Charges enter on lines 103, Section J and 502 Section K $ 11,670.81			$ 321.58

LOCAL TAXES: $ 99.20   COUNTY TAXES: $106.63   SCHOOL TAXES: $780.86   TOTAL: $986.69

I have carefully reviewed the HUD-1 Settlement Statement and, to the best of my knowledge and belief, it is a true and accurate statement of all receipts and disbursements made on my account or by me in this transaction. I further certify that I have received a copy of the HUD-1 Settlement Statement.

BORROWER/BUYER _____   SELLER _____
Kevin Bell   Patrick Marino

BORROWER/BUYER_____   SELLER _____
                                                                        Carol Marino

The HUD-1 Settlement Statement which I have prepared is a true and accurate account of this transaction. I have caused the funds to be disbursed in accordance with this statement.

_____09/03/2003

WARNING: It is a crime to knowingly make false statements to the United States in this or any other similar form. Penalties upon conviction can include a fine and imprisonment. For details see: Title 18 U.S. Code Sec. 1001 and 1010.

APPENDIX III

RENT TO OWN

LEASE OPTION AGREEMENT

THIS AGREEMENT is made by and between:_____
(hereinafter called "Owner"),
and_____(hereinafter called "Buyer").

1. OPTION. In consideration of the sum of $_____ (the
    "Option Fee") paid by Buyer, seller grants to Buyer the Option to
    purchase the Property located at _____
    _____("the Property").
    The Option may be exercised at any time during the Option Period.
    The Option Period is the same as the term of the Lease between
    Owner and Tenant dated_____ (the "Lease"). To
    exercise the Option, Buyer will give seller written notice, during the
    Option Period, of Buyer's election to exercise the Option. This notice
    will be directed to Seller at the above address or any other address
    designated by Seller in writing. If Buyer exercises the Option, Buyer
    shall purchase the Property within the terms set forth in this
    Agreement.

2. PRICE: The Purchase Price shall be_____,
    payable as follows:

    a. If Buyer has fully performed all covenants and conditions of this
        Option Agreement and the Lease in a timely manner, Buyer will
        receive the following credits:

        i.   The Option Fee will be applied to the purchase price at the
             time of Closing, but will not be refunded if Buyer does not
             exercise this Option and buy the Property.

        ii. Buyer will receive a credit in the amount of $_____ per
             month for each rent payment if the full amount is made in a
             timely manner in accordance with the Lease.

3. INCLUDED IN THE PURCHASE: The property shall also include all
    land, together with all improvements thereon, all appurtenant rights,
    privileges, easements, buildings, fixtures, heating, electrical, air
    conditioning fixtures and facilities, window shades, Venetian blinds,
    awnings, curtain rods, screens, storm windows and doors, affixed
    mirrors, wall-to-wall carpeting, stair carpeting, built-in kitchen
    appliances, bathroom fixtures, radio and television aerials,

landscaping and shrubbery, water softeners, garage door openers and operating devices, and all utility or storage buildings or sheds.

The property shall also include any oven/range and refrigerator located on the premises at the time Tenant took possession of the premises; however, the condition of these appliances is not warranted and are conveyed "AS IS".

4. SETTLEMENT. Settlement will be held in Allegheny County, Pennsylvania. Settlement will be within thirty days of the exercise of the option. If settlement is not completed by this date either party will then have the right to declare time to be of the essence by giving notice to the other party. The notice will state that time is of the essence and will fix the time, date and place of settlement. The date fixed may not be earlier than 15 days or later than 30 days following the effective date of giving such notice.

5. INSPECTION. Prior to exercising the Option Buyer will have occupied the Property and inspected the Property fully. If Buyer purchases the Property, Buyer will take the Property "AS IS" with all faults, known or unknown. Buyer assumes the risk of any unknown defects to the property.

6. PRORATION ITEMS. (A) real estate transfer taxes will be shared equally between Seller and Buyer; (B) current water and sewer charges, municipal garbage and rubbish removal charges, rents, interest and real estate taxes will be paid by Buyer; and (C) real estate taxes will be prorated on a calendar year basis for the calendar year of settlement based upon real estate taxes levied or estimated to be levied in that year by each taxing body without regard to the date of the levy or the fiscal year of the taxing body. Unless this Property is located in the City of Pittsburgh, real estate taxes levied by the local School District will be prorated on a fiscal year from July 1 through June 30.

7. SELLER'S EXPENSE. Seller will pay the cost of deed preparation, title clearance.

8. POSSESSION. Possession of the Property will be delivered to Buyer pursuant to the Lease.

9. RISK OF LOSS; INSURANCE. Risk of loss of the Property will remain upon Seller until Buyer takes possession of the Property.

Buyer may have an insurable interest in the Property upon the signing of this Agreement. To protect Buyer's own interest, Buyer should have adequate fire and casualty insurance with extended coverage on the Property to protect Buyer's interest.

10. MAINTENANCE OF THE PROPERTY; BUYER'S OPTION. Buyer will maintain and make all repairs needed to keep the property in as good condition as it is now.

11. EMINENT DOMAIN; BUYER'S OPTION. If any part of the property is taken by eminent domain before settlement, Seller will notify Buyer of the taking within 5 days, but not later than the settlement. Buyer will have the option to proceed with this Agreement and pay the balance of the purchase price, and Seller will assign to Buyer the award, if any, to which Seller may be entitled. To exercise this option Buyer will give notice to Seller before settlement. If Buyer fails to give the notice, Buyer will be conclusively deemed to have chosen option (B).

12. MUNICIPAL IMPROVEMENTS. Seller will pay any municipal claim against the Property if the ordinance or resolution authorizing the work or improvement is adopted prior to the date of this Agreement. Buyer will pay any municipal claim against the Property if the ordinance or resolution authorizing the work or improvement is adopted on or after the date of this Agreement.

13. DEFAULT.
    a. By Buyer. If Buyer defaults, Seller may retain any credits or money paid by Buyer as liquidated damages.
    b. By Seller. If Seller defaults Buyer's sole remedy is to bring an action for specific performance and return of the Option Fee and rental credits.

14. UNDER AND SUBJECT: Buyer will take title to the Property subject to the following so long as they do not adversely affect the present use of the Property or at any time require removal or alteration of existing improvements: (A) building and use restrictions of record; (B) vehicular or pedestrian easements of record affecting the Property and being along the front, rear or side lot lines; (C) water, sewer, gas, electric, cable television, and telephone lines or easements therefor of record or as presently installed; (D) prior grants, reservations or leases or coal, oil, gas or other minerals as shown by instruments of record; and (E) easements apparent upon inspection of the Property.

15. ZONING AND OTHER ORDINANCES. Seller warrants that: Property has the following Zoning Classification, Residential.

16. INSPECTION OF PROPERTY. Buyer represents that Buyer has occupied and inspected the Property before exercising the Option. Buyer is relying only on the inspection of the Property made by Buyer and is not relying on any oral statement concerning the physical condition of the Property given to Buyer by Seller or any Broker except for written statements contained in this Agreement.

17. SEWAGE FACILITY NOTICE. The property is serviced by a community sewage system.

18. COAL NOTICE. NOTICE THIS DOCUMENT MAY NOT SELL, CONVEY, TRANSFER, INCLUDE OR INSURE THE TITLE TO THE COAL AND RIGHT TO SUPPORT UNDERNEATH THE SURFACE LAND DESCRIBED OR REFERRED TO HEREIN, AND THE OWNER OR OWNERS OF SUCH COAL MAY HAVE THE COMPLETE LEGAL RIGHT TO REMOVE ALL OF SUCH COAL AND IN THAT CONNECTION, DAMAGE MAY RESULT TO THE SURFACE OF THE LAND AND ANY HOUSE, BUILDING OR OTHER STRUCTURE ON OR IN SUCH LAND. THE INCLUSION OF THIS NOTICE DOES NOT ENLARGE, RESTRICT OR MODIFY ANY LEGAL RIGHTS OR ESTATES OTHERWISE CREATED, TRANSFERRED, EXCEPTED OR RESERVED BY THIS INSTRUMENT. (This notice is set forth in the manner provided in Section 1 of the Act of July 17, 1957, P.L. 984, as amended, and is not intended as notice of unrecorded instruments, if any.) Unless this notice is stricken, the deed for the Property will contain this notice and will also contain, and, Buyer will sign, the notice specified in the Bituminous Mine Subsidence and Land Conservation Act of 1966.

19. NOTICE TO PARTIES. Any notice given by Seller to Buyer or by Buyer to Seller will be in writing. Any notices will be delivered either in the manner provided by law for the service of process in equity or by certified or registered mail to the receiving party at the address for the receiving party which appears on the first page of this Agreement. Any mailed notice will be deemed delivered to the receiving party on the second business day after mailing occurs.

20. COVENANT NOT TO RECORD. Buyer will not record this Agreement, and any recording of this Agreement by Buyer will

constitute a default by Buyer under this Agreement and render this Agreement null and void.

21. BINDING EFFECT. Seller and Buyer intend to be legally bound by this Agreement. All of its terms and conditions will extend to and be binding upon the parties to this Agreement and upon their respective heirs, executors, administrators, personal representatives, successors and assigns. This Agreement may not be assigned by the Buyer without the written notice of Seller.

22. INTERPRETATION. This Agreement and the Lease constitute the entire contract between the parties and there are no other understandings, oral or written, relating to the sale and purchase of the Property. This Agreement may not be changed, modified, or amended, in whole or in part, except in another writing, signed by all parties. Wherever used in this Agreement, the singular will include the plural, the plural the singular, and the use of any gender will be applicable to all genders. Paragraph headings and italicized clauses are inserted for convenience only and will not form part of the text of this Agreement.

23. LEAD WARNING STATEMENT AND WAIVER. Every purchaser of any interest in residential real property on which a residential dwelling was built prior to 1978 is notified that such property may present exposure to lead from lead-based paint that may place young children at risk of developing lead poisoning, Lead poisoning in young children may produce permanent neurological damage, including learning disabilities, reduced intelligence quotient, behavioral problems, and impaired memory. Lead poisoning also presents a particular risk to pregnant women. The seller of any interest in residential real property is required to provide the buyer with any information on lead-based paint hazards from risk assessments or inspections in the seller's possession and notify the buyer of any known lead-based paint hazards. A risk assessment or inspection for possible lead-based paid hazards is recommended before purchase.

Tenant/Buyer hereby waives the opportunity to conduct a risk assessment or inspection for the presence of lead-based paint and/or lead-based paint hazards.

THIS IS A LEGALLY BINDING CONTRACT. IF NOT FULLY UNDERSTOOD, CONSULT YOUR ATTORNEY PRIOR TO SIGNING.

IN WITNESS WHEREOF, the parties hereto have set their hands to this Option to Purchase as of this date: _____, 20____.

_____   _____
Witness   Buyer

_____   _____
Witness   Buyer

WITNESS:

_____   By: _____

RESIDENTIAL LEASE AGREEMENT

NOTICE TO TENANT: WHEN TENANT SIGNS THIS LEASE, TENANT MAY GIVE UP CERTAIN IMPORTANT CONSUMER RIGHTS. IF TENANT DOES NOT MEET LEASE RESPONSIBILITIES, TENANT MAY LOSE TENANT'S SECURITY DEPOSIT. LANDLORD MAY ALSO SUE TENANT IN COURT FOR RENT, DAMAGES AND TO GET THE APARTMENT BACK. TENANT MAY LOSE TENANT'S PERSONAL PROPERTY.

IF THE LANDLORD WINS (GETS A MONEY JUDGMENT AGAINST THE TENANT), THE LANDLORD CAN USE THE COURT PROCESS TO TAKE THE TENANT(S) PERSONAL GOODS, FURNITURE, MOTOR VEHICLES AND MONEY IN BANKS.

The LANDLORD and TENANT agree to lease the APARTMENT under the following terms and conditions:

LANDLORD _____

TENANT _____

LEASED PROPERTY _____

LEASE TERMS:
Date of this Lease _____

Monthly Rent _____

Security Deposit_____

This Lease Begins on_____and Ends at 5 p.m. on_____

1. PAYMENT OF RENT: TENANT must pay rent on or before the_____ day of each month (the "Monthly Due Date") without LANDLORD having to ask or demand payment.

2. LATE CHARGE: If TENANT pays rent within _____ days after the Monthly Due Date TENANT will pay a late charge of $_____ PER DAY FOR EVERY DAY THAT THE RENT IS LATE.

If TENANT uses a check to pay rent, TENANT shall make rent payable to _____

All rent must be delivered to LANDLORD at LANDLORD's address. TENANT agrees to write TENANT's apartment number on all rent checks.

3. WHERE TO PAY/SEND RENT. TENANT must deliver or mail each rent payment to LANDLORD's address for Rent Payment and Notices. If TENANT properly mails rent, receipt by LANDLORD is the second business day after the U.S. Postal Service Postmark.

4. PAYMENT IN FULL. TENANT must pay rent in full. TENANT must pay the first month's rent before TENANT moves into the . PROPERTY. LANDLORD may also require TENANT to pay any part of a month's rent if this LEASE does not begin on the first day of a month.

5. ASSIGNMENT/SUBLETTING. TENANT may not rent the APARTMENT to another person unless LANDLORD agrees in writing in advance. If LANDLORD agrees to permit/allow TENANT to rent the APARTMENT to another person, then:

   (A) TENANT shall remain responsible for the performance of all of TENANT's responsibilities under this LEASE, including the payment of rent; and
   (B) The person who rents the APARTMENT from the TENANT must agree to take on the responsibilities for the APARTMENT as required by LANDLORD.

6. ADDITIONAL RENT. Additional rent is payable as rent with the regular rent next due. TENANT must pay as additional rent the cost to repair any damages to the PROPERTY. TENANT must also pay as additional rent all utility charges for the PROPERTY.

7. REPAIRS. Tenant has inspected the premises and agrees to lease said premises "as-is", except as follows:

NO EXCEPTIONS

TENANT agrees that the PROPERTY is in good order and repair. TENANT agrees to immediately tell LANDLORD of any condition of the PROPERTY that is not in good order or repair.

TENANT agrees to pay to repair any damage to the PROPERTY for damage caused by TENANT or the family or visitors of TENANT. If repairs are not completed within a reasonable time, LANDLORD may pay to have the repair completed. This cost is considered additional rent and due with the following month's payment.

TENANT shall make all necessary repairs to keep the PROPERTY in a habitable condition. For all repairs except emergency repairs, TENANT must first get written approval from LANDLORD before TENANT repairs.

TENANT agrees to pay to open all clogged sewers, drains, toilets, sinks and traps, or reimburse LANDLORD for these costs.

8. APPLIANCES. Any appliances provided by the LANDLORD are the property of the LANDLORD. However, replacement and repair of said appliances are the responsibility of the TENANT.

9. LANDLORD RESPONSIBILITY. LANDLORD is not responsible for any of the following:

   (A) Any damage or injury to TENANT or to the family, employees or visitors of TENANT; or

   (B) Any damage or loss to any property of TENANT in or near the PROPERTY.

10. TENANT'S PROPERTY AND INSURANCE. LANDLORD does not insure TENANT's personal property. TENANT should purchase insurance to:

    (A) Insure TENANT's personal property; and

    (B) Insure against claims for casualty or personal injury.

11. PETS. TENANT may not keep any animals, birds or pets of any kind in the PROPERTY. If TENANT wants to keep a pet in the PROPERTY, TENANT must:

    (A) First get the written permission from LANDLORD; and

    (B) Pay LANDLORD an additional pet fee as determined by LANDLORD.

12. STATEMENTS IN TENANT'S APPLICATION. TENANT has completed an application before the beginning of this LEASE. Only those persons named in the application may live in the PROPERTY. If any information in TENANT's application is misleading, incorrect or untrue, then LANDLORD has the right to end/cancel this LEASE. No spoken statements made by LANDLORD's employees are a part of this LEASE.

13. UTILITIES. TENANT will pay all utility charges. If LANDLORD pays any utility charges, TENANT will reimburse LANDLORD.

14. WHEN PROPERTY IS AVAILABLE. LANDLORD is not responsible if LANDLORD is unable to give TENANT possession of the PROPERTY on the date LANDLORD promised. TENANT shall begin to pay rent only when possession is available.

    The LEASE begins on the day TENANT is given possession of the PROPERTY. The ending date of this LEASE will not change.

    If LANDLORD is unable to give possession of the PROPERTY on the date the LANDLORD promised, LANDLORD will tell TENANT immediately. If the delay is for TEN (10) days or less, TENANT must wait to take possession. If the delay is for more than TEN (10) days, TENANT may obtain a full refund and this LEASE is canceled.

15. USE. TENANT agrees to use the PROPERTY only as a private residence. The maximum number of people allowed to live in the PROPERTY are _____ adults and _____ children. TENANT agrees not to use the PROPERTY:

    (A) In a way that violates any local, county, state or federal law.

    (B) In a way that interferes with the comfort or rights of others. This means that annoying sounds, smells and lights are not allowed.

16. CHARGES FOR RETURNED CHECKS. TENANT agrees to pay LANDLORD a check handling charge of $25.00 each time a check written to LANDLORD by TENANT is returned for insufficient funds (NSF); or for any other reason.

    Once LANDLORD receives a returned rent check from TENANT, LANDLORD may require all future payments in cash, money order or cashier's check.

17. SECURITY DEPOSIT. TENANT must pay LANDLORD a security deposit in the amount of _____ along with the first payment of rent. TENANT agrees that the security deposit is not a prepayment of rent and is not the last month's rent.

18. LANDLORD has the right to deduct the following from TENANT'S security deposit:

    (A) Any unpaid rents and utility charges; and

    (B) Any unpaid charges and check handling charges; and

    (C) Any attorney fees, court costs and other costs which LANDLORD must pay because TENANT does not follow this LEASE; and

    (D) All carpet cleaning charges beyond reasonable wear and tear; and

    (E) The cost to make any repairs or replacements to any fixture, system or appliance damaged or abused by TENANT in the PROPERTY; and

    (F) The amount which LANDLORD must pay to restore the PROPERTY to its original condition, but not to correct reasonable wear and tear to the PROPERTY; and

    (G) LANDLORD's reasonable costs to clean the PROPERTY if TENANT does not leave the PROPERTY in clean and rentable condition when this LEASE ends; and

    (H) The amount LANDLORD must pay to remove all debris, rubbish or trash TENANT leaves in or around the PROPERTY; and

    (I) The amount LANDLORD must pay to replace keys for the PROPERTY which TENANT does not return to LANDLORD at the end of the LEASE.

    So long as TENANT gives LANDLORD TENANT'S forwarding address in writing, LANDLORD will return the Security Deposit to TENANT, minus any necessary deductions.

Within thirty (30) days after the end of the LEASE, TENANT must give LANDLORD TENANT'S forwarding address in writing.

19. TENANT REMODELING. LANDLORD must approve in advance any plan of TENANT:

    (A) To remodel, paint or make any change in the PROPERTY; or

    (B) To add or remove any appliance or other permanent fixture of the PROPERTY.

20. LANDLORD'S ACCESS TO THE PROPERTY. LANDLORD may enter the PROPERTY without TENANT's permission after reasonable notice under the following circumstances:

    (A) To do routine maintenance; and

    (B) To show the PROPERTY to prospective tenants, appraisers or purchasers.

    LANDLORD may enter the PROPERTY without TENANT's permission and without notice to respond to an emergency.

21. LOCKS AND KEYS. LANDLORD will provide a lock for the outside door(s) of the PROPERTY. The lock shall meet the safety standards generally applied to residences near the PROPERTY.

    TENANT shall not place any other lock on any doors of the PROPERTY. TENANT shall return to LANDLORD all keys to the PROPERTY on the last day of this LEASE. LANDLORD must at all times have a key to the PROPERTY.

22. FIRE HAZARDS. TENANT may not do anything in or near the PROPERTY that might cause a fire or that will increase the amount paid by LANDLORD for insurance for the PROPERTY. No flammable material is allowed.

    TENANT must give LANDLORD immediate notice of fire, accident, damage, or dangerous condition in the PROPERTY. If the TENANT cannot use the PROPERTY because of fire or other mishap, TENANT is not required to pay rent for the time the PROPERTY is unusable (as long as not caused by TENANT).

If the PROPERTY is unusable because of fire or other mishap, LANDLORD may cancel/end the LEASE. If LANDLORD decides to end the LEASE, LANDLORD will notify TENANT within 30 days of the fire or mishap. If not, LANDLORD shall have a reasonable time to repair.

If a fire or mishap is caused by an act or failure to act by TENANT, then TENANT makes and pays for all repairs. TENANT must still pay the full rent with no adjustment. This applies to TENANT's family, employee, guest or visitor.

23. INSURANCE. TENANT agrees to purchase insurance at TENANT's expense sufficient to protect TENANT and TENANT's property against fire, theft, burglary, breakage, and all other hazards. TENANT understands that any insurance policy carried by the LANDLORD covers damage to the premises only, and acknowledges that neither LANDLORD nor LANDLORD's insurance provider is liable for any loss of TENANT's personal property.

24. ORDER IN WHICH RENT PAYMENT IS APPLIED. Rent received is first applied to monies due from the past in the following order:

   (A) Charges, Fees and Check Handling Charges

   (B) TENANT Owed Utility Bills

   (C) Legal and Court Costs

   (D) Past Rent Due

   (E) Current Rent

25. LEAD BASE PAINT NOTICE

   (A) All landlords of buildings constructed before 1978 must supply to their tenants the disclosure statement required by the Lead Base Paint Hazard Act.

   (B) If the PROPERTY is older than 1978, LANDLORD, TENANT and Agent (if any) must sign the attached Lead-Based Paint Disclosure Statement.

26. ENDING THIS LEASE. Either LANDLORD or TENANT may end this LEASE at the end of the term. Either may do so by giving the other party written notice no less than sixty (60) days before the end of the LEASE.

    If neither party gives notice to end this LEASE, then this LEASE is extended for a term of one (1) month.

    Other than the length of the term, the extended LEASE term shall have the same terms and conditions as this LEASE.

    LANDLORD may wish to extend the LEASE but increase the rent. LANDLORD must give TENANT notice of the proposed increase at least sixty (60) days before the end of the LEASE.

    TENANT then has thirty (30) days to give LANDLORD written notice of TENANT's decision to reject the offer at the increased rent.

    If TENANT rejects the increased rent offer, then this LEASE will end on the last day of this LEASE. If TENANT has not responded within thirty (30) days after LANDLORD's notice, the increase will automatically take effect at the beginning of the new LEASE term.

    If this LEASE is a month-to-month LEASE, then either LANDLORD or TENANT may end this LEASE at the end of the term. Either may do so by giving the other party written notice no less than thirty (30) days before the end of the LEASE.

27. LEAVING THE PROPERTY BEFORE THE LEASE ENDS. If TENANT leaves the PROPERTY before this LEASE ends, TENANT remains responsible to pay all rent:

    (A) For the remaining term of this LEASE; or

    (B) Until LANDLORD rents the PROPERTY to another person, whichever happens first.

    If LANDLORD rents the PROPERTY to another person, TENANT shall pay LANDLORD the cost of preparing the PROPERTY for rent and finding another tenant.

28. ATTORNEY FEES. If LANDLORD hires an attorney to represent LANDLORD because TENANT breaks any agreement made in this LEASE, TENANT shall pay:

(A) the reasonable fees of LANDLORD's attorney; and

(B) any court costs.

29. STAYING AFTER LEASE ENDS. If this LEASE ends for any reason and TENANT remains in the PROPERTY, then LANDLORD shall have the right to go to court to remove TENANT and TENANT's possessions from the PROPERTY.

30. ENTIRE AGREEMENT. This LEASE is the complete statement of the agreement between LANDLORD and TENANT regarding the PROPERTY. This LEASE can only change by a written agreement signed by LANDLORD and TENANT. LANDLORD and TENANT agree to give all notices in writing to LANDLORD or TENANT either personally, by First Class U.S. Mail or by certified mail.

31. TENANT GIVES UP THE RIGHT TO NOTICE. BY SIGNING THIS LEASE, TENANT GIVES UP OR WAIVES ALL NOTICE WHICH TENANT IS ENTITLED TO UNDER THE LANDLORD AND TENANT ACT OF PENNSYLVANIA.

32. TENANT VIOLATES THIS LEASE IF TENANT:

    (A) Fails to pay rent or other charges to LANDLORD on time; or

    (B) Leaves (abandons) the PROPERTY without the LANDLORD's permission before the end of the LEASE; or

    (C) Does not leave the PROPERTY at the end of the LEASE; or

    (D) Does not do all the things that TENANT agreed to do in this LEASE.

33. IF TENANT VIOLATES THE LEASE, EACH TENANT AGREES TO WAIVE NOTICE TO QUIT. THIS MEANS THAT THE LANDLORD MAY FILE A COMPLAINT IN COURT ASKING FOR AN ORDER EVICTING EACH TENANT FROM THE PROPERTY WITHOUT GIVING EACH TENANT NOTICE TO VACATE FIRST. THE LANDLORD CAN ONLY EVICT TENANT BY COURT ACTION.

34. SIGNATURES. Each TENANT who signs this LEASE is fully responsible for the full amount of rent and all of TENANT's responsibilities that are in this LEASE.

WITNESS: LANDLORD:

_____   By: _____

WITNESS   TENANT:

_____   _____

_____   _____

CREDIT REPORTING AGENCIES

Equifax

www.equifax.com
P.O. Box 740241
Atlanta, GA 30374
1-800-685-1111

Experian

www.experian.com
P.O. Box 9595
Allen, TX 75013
1-888-397-3742

Trans Union Corp.

www.transunion.com
P.O. Box 1000
Chester, PA 19022-1000
1-800-916-8800

www.myfico.com

UNIFORM RESIDENTIAL LOAN APPLICATION

This application is designed to be completed by the applicant(s) with the lender's assistance. Applicants should complete this form as "Borrower" or "Co-Borrower", as applicable. Co-Borrower information must also be provided (and the appropriate box checked) when the ____ income or assets of a person other than the "Borrower" (including the Borrower's spouse) will be used as a basis for loan qualification or ____ the income or assets of the Borrower's spouse will not be used as a basis for loan qualification, but his or her liabilities must be considered because the Borrower resides in a community property state, the security property is located in a community property state, or the Borrower is relying on other property located in a community property state as a basis for repayment of the loan.

I. TYPE OF MORTGAGE AND TERMS OF LOAN

Mortgage Applied for ____ V.A. ____ Conventional ____ Other

____ FHA ____ FmHA

Agency Case Number   Lender Case Number

Amount $ Interest Rate ____ %   No. of Months

Amortization Type: ____ Fixed Rate ____ Other (explain)

____ GPM ____ ARM (type)

II. PROPERTY INFORMATION AND PURPOSE OF LOAN

Subject Property Address (street, city, state, ZIP)   No. of Units

Legal Description of Subject Property (attach description if necessary)   Year Built

Purpose of Loan ____ Purchase ____ Construction ____ Other (explain)

____ Refinance ____ Construction-Permanent

Property will be:

____ Primary Residence ____ Secondary Residence ____ Investment

Complete this line if construction or construction-permanent loan.

Year lot Acquired   Original Cost $ Amount Existing Liens $ (a) Present Value of Lot $ (b) Cost of Improvements $ Total (a+b) $

Complete this line if this is a refinance loan.

Year Acquired $ Original Cost $ Amount Existing Liens $ Purpose of Refinance   Describe improvements ____ made ____ to be made

Cost $

Title will be held in what Name(s)

Manner in which Title will be held

Estate will be held in:
___ Fee Simple
___ Leasehold
(show expiration date)

Source of Down Payment, Settlement Charges and/or Subordinate Financing (explain)

III. BORROWER INFORMATION

Borrower	Co-Borrower
Borrower's Name (include Jr. or. Sr. if applicable)	Co-Borrower's Name (include Jr. or Sr. if applicable)
Social Security No. Home Phone Age Yrs school	Social Security No. Home Phone Age Yrs school
___ Married ___ Unmarried (include single, divorced, widowed) Dependents (not listed by Co-Borrower) No. Ages	___ Married ___ Unmarried (include single, divorced, widowed) Dependents (not listed by Borrower) No. Ages
___ Separated	___ Separated
Present Address (street, city, state, ZIP) ___ Own ___ Rent ___ No. Yrs	Present Address (street, city, state, ZIP) ___ Own ___ Rent ___ No. Yrs.

If residing at present address for less than two years, complete the following:

| Former Address (street, city, state, ZIP)   ___ Own ___ Rent   ___ No. Yrs | Former Address (street, city, state, ZIP)   ___ Own ___ Rent   ___ No. Yrs. |
| Former Address (street, city, state, ZIP)   ___ Own ___ Rent   ___ No. Yrs | Former Address (street, city, state, ZIP)   ___ Own ___ Rent   ___ No. Yrs. |

IV. EMPLOYMENT INFORMATION

	Borrower		Co-Borrower	

Name and Address of Employer ___ Self-employed Name and Address of Employer ___ Self-employed

___ Yrs on this job

___ Yrs employed in this line of work/profession

Position/Title/Type of Business Business Phone

If employed in current position for less than two years or if currently employed in more than one position, complete the following:

Name and Address of Employer ___ Self-employed Dates (from-to) ___ Monthly Income

Position/Title/Type of Business Business Phone

Name and Address of Employer ___ Self-employed Dates (from-to) ___ Monthly Income

Position/Title/Type of Business Business Phone

V. MONTHLY INCOME AND COMBINED HOUSING EXPENSE INFORMATION

Gross Monthly Income	Borrower	Co-Borrower	Total	Combined Monthly Housing Expense	Present	Proposed
Base Empl. Income*	$	$	$	Rent	$	
Overtime				First Mortgage (P&I)		
Bonuses				Other Financing (P&I)		

Commissions
Dividends/Interest
Net Rental Income
Other (before completing see the notice in "describe other income" below)

Hazard Insurance
Real Estate Taxes
Mortgage Insurance
Homeowner Assn dues
Other

TOTAL $

TOTAL $

$

*Self-Employed Borrower(s) may be required to provide additional documentation such as tax returns and financial statements.

DESCRIBE OTHER INCOME   Notice: Alimony, child support, or separate maintenance income need not be revealed if the Borrower (B) or Co-Borrower (C) does not choose to have it considered for repaying this loan.

B/C   Monthly Amt
                                       $

VI. ASSETS AND LIABILITIES

This statement and any applicable supporting schedules may be completed jointly by both married and unmarried Co-Borrowers if their assets and liabilities are sufficiently joined so that the Statement can be meaningfully and fairly presented on a combined basis, otherwise separate Statements and Schedules are required. If the Co-Borrower section was completed about a spouse, this Statement and supporting schedules must be completed about that spouse also.

Completed _____ Jointly _____ Not Jointly

ASSETS

Description   Cash or Market Value
Cash deposit toward purchase held by: $

List checking and savings accounts below

Name and address of Bank, S&L or Credit Union _____

Account No. _____ $ _____

Name and address of Bank, S&L or Credit Union _____

Account No. _____ $ _____

Name and address of Bank, S&L or Credit Union _____

Account No. _____ $ _____

Name and address of Bank, S&L or Credit Union _____

Account No. _____ $ _____

Stocks & Bonds (Company name/number & description) _____ $ _____

Life insurance net cash value _____

Face amount $ _____ $ _____

SUBTOTAL LIQUID ASSETS $ _____

Real estate owned (enter market value from schedule of real estate owned) $ _____

Vested interest in retirement fund $ _____

Net worth of business(es) owned (attach financial statement) $ _____

Automobiles owned (make and year) _____ $ _____

Other assets (itemize) _____ $ _____

TOTAL ASSETS a. $ _____

LIABILITIES

Liabilities and Pledged Assets. List the creditor's name, address and account number for all outstanding debts, including automobile loans, revolving charge accounts, real estate loans, alimony, child support, stock pledges, etc. Use continuation sheet, if necessary. Indicate by (*) those liabilities which will be satisfied upon sale of real estate owned or upon refinancing of the subject property.

LIABILITIES	Monthly Payment and Mos. Left to Pay	Unpaid Balance
Name and address of Company	$ Payt./Mos.	$
Acct. No.		
Name and address of Company	$ Payt./Mos.	$
Acct. No.		
Name and address of Company	$ Payt./Mos.	$
Acct. No.		
Name and address of Company	$ Payt./Mos.	$
Acct. No.		
Name and address of Company	$ Payt./Mos.	$
Acct. No.		

Name and address of Company $ Payt./Mos. $

Acct. No.

Name and address of Company $ Payt./Mos. $

Acct. No.

Alimony/Child Support/Separate Maintenance Payments Owed to: $

Job Related Expense (child care, union dues, etc.) $

Total Monthly Payments $

Net Worth (a-b) $ Total Liabilities $

Schedule of Real Estate Owned: (if additional properties are owned, use continuation sheet)

Property address (enter S if sold, PS if pending sale or R if rental being held for income)	Type of Property	Present Market Value	Amount of Mortgage & Liens	Gross Rental Income	Mortgage Payments	Insurance Maintenance Taxes & Misc	Net Rental Income
		$	$				
		$	$	$	$	$	$

List any additional names under which credit has previously been received and indicate appropriate creditor name(s) and account number(s):

Alternate Name	Creditor Name	Account Number

VII. DETAILS OF TRANSACTION

a. Purchase price $
b. Alterations, improvements, repairs
c. Land (if acquired separately)
d. Refinance (incl. debts to be paid off)
e. Estimated prepaid items
f. Estimated closing costs
g. PMI, MIP, Funding Fee
h. Discount (if Borrower will pay)
i. TOTAL COSTS (add items a through l)
j. Subordinate financing
k. Borrower's closing cost paid by Seller
l. Other Credits (explain)

m. Loan amount (exclude PMI, MIP, Funding Fee financed)
n. PMI, MIP, Funding Fee financed
o. Loan amount (add m & n)
p. Cash from/to Borrower

VIII. DECLARATIONS

If you answer "yes" to any questions a through l, please use continuation sheet for explanation.

	Borrower		Co-Borrower	
	Yes	No	Yes	No
a. Are there any outstanding judgments against you?	—	—	—	—
b. Have you been declared bankrupt within the past 7 years?	—	—	—	—
c. Have you had property foreclosed upon or given title or deed in lieu thereof in the last 7 years?	—	—	—	—
d. Are you a party to a lawsuit?	—	—	—	—
e. Have you directly or indirectly been obligated on any loan which resulted in foreclosure, transfer of title in lieu of foreclosure or judgment? (This would include such loans as home mortgage loans, SBA loans, home improvement loans, educational loans, manufactured (mobile) home loans, any mortgage, financial obligation, bond, or loan guarantee. If "Yes", provide details, including date, name and address of Lender, FHA or VA case number, if any, and reasons for the action.)	—			
f. Are you presently delinquent or in default on any Federal debt or any other loan, mortgage, financial obligation, bond, or loan guarantee? If "Yes", give details as described in the preceding question.	—	—	—	—
g. Are you obligated to pay alimony, child support, or separate maintenance?	—	—	—	—
h. Is any part of the down payment borrowed?	—	—	—	—
i. Are you a co-maker or endorser on a note?	—	—	—	—
j. Are you a U.S. Citizen?	—	—	—	—
k. Are you a permanent resident alien?	—	—	—	—
l. Do you intend to occupy the property as your primary residence? If "Yes", complete question m below.	—	—	—	—

m. Have you had an ownership interest in a property in the last three years?

   (1)   What type of property did you own—principal residence (PR), second home (SH), or investment property (IP)?

   (2)   How did you hold title to the home—solely by yourself (S), jointly with your spouse (SP), or jointly with another person (O)?

IX. ACKNOWLEDGMENT AND AGREEMENT

The undersigned specifically acknowledge(s) and agree(s) that: (1) the loan requested by this application will be secured by a first mortgage or deed of trust on the property described herein; (2) the property will not be used for any illegal or prohibited purpose or use; (3) all statements made in this application are made for the purpose of obtaining the loan indicated herein; (4) occupation of the property will be as indicated above; (5) verification or reverification of any information contained in the application may be made at any time by the Lender, its agents, successors and assigns, either directly or through a credit reporting agency, from any source named in this application, and the original copy of this application will be retained by the Lender, even if the loan is not approved; (6) the Lender, its agents, successors and assigns will rely on the information contained in the application and I/we have a continuing obligation to amend and/or supplement the information provided in this application if any of the material facts which I/we have represented herein should change prior to closing; (7) in the event my/our payments on the loan indicated in this application become delinquent, the Lender, its agents, successors and assigns, may, in addition to all their other rights and remedies, report my/our name(s) and account information to a credit reporting agency; (8) ownership of the loan may be transferred to successor or assign of the Lender without notice to me and/or the administration of the loan account may be transferred to an agent, successor or assign of the Lender with prior notice to me; (9) the Lender, its agents, successors and assigns make no representations or warranties, express or implied, to the Borrower(s) regarding the property, the condition of the property, or the value of the property.

Certification: I/We certify that the information provided in this application is true and correct as of the date set forth opposite my/our signature(s) on this application and acknowledge my/our understanding that any intentional or negligent misrepresentation(s) of the information contained in this application may result in civil liability and/or criminal penalties including, but not limited to, fine or imprisonment or both under the provisions of Title 18, United States Code, Section 1001, et seq. And liability for monetary damages to the Lender, its agents, successors and assigns, insurers and any other person who may suffer any loss due to reliance upon any misrepresentation which I/we have made on this application.

Borrower's Signature   Date   Co-Borrower's Signature   Date

X. INFORMATION FOR GOVERNMENT MONITORING PURPOSES

The following information is requested by the Federal Government for certain types of loans related to a dwelling in order to monitor the Lender's compliance with equal credit opportunity, fair housing and home mortgage disclosure laws. You are not required to furnish this information, but are encouraged to do so. The law provides that a Lender may neither discriminate on the basis of this information, nor on whether you choose to furnish it. However, if you choose not to furnish it under Federal regulations this Lender is required to note race and sex on the basis of visual observation or surname. If you do not wish to furnish the above information, please check the box below. (Lender must review the above material to assure that the disclosure satisfies all requirements to which the Lender is subject under applicable state law for the particular type of loan applied for.)

BORROWER

Race/National Origin:
_____ I do not wish to furnish this information
_____ American Indian or Alaskan Native
_____ Asian or Pacific Islander
_____ Black, not of Hispanic origin
_____ Hispanic
_____ White, not of Hispanic origin
_____ Other (specify) _____

Sex: _____ Female _____ Male

CO-BORROWER

Race/National Origin:
_____ I do not wish to furnish this information
_____ American Indian or Alaskan Native
_____ Asian or Pacific Islander
_____ Black, not of Hispanic origin
_____ Hispanic
_____ White, not of Hispanic origin
_____ Other (specify) _____

Sex: _____ Female _____ Male

To be Complete by Interviewer
This application was taken by:
_____ face-to-face interview
_____ by mail
_____ by telephone

Interviewer's Name

Interviewer's Signature

Interviewer's phone number

Name and Address Interviewer's Employer

COMMUNITY INVESTMENT SERVICES
1 Oxford Ctr., Ste. 450
Pittsburgh, PA 15219
(P)412-777-9892 (F)412-777-3281

INDEX